Data Distributions

Describing Variability and Comparing Groups

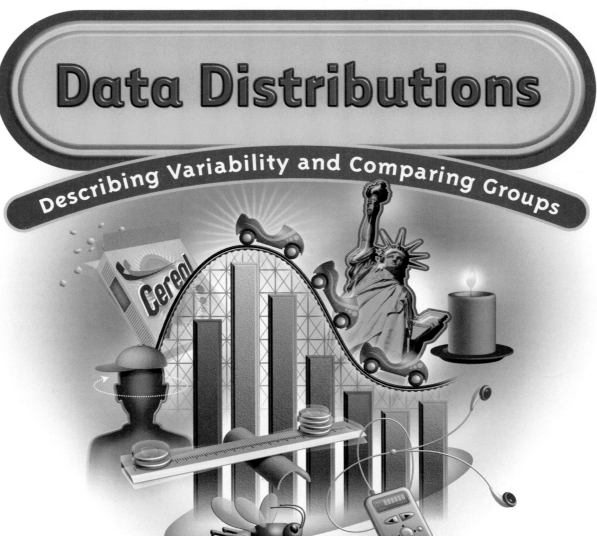

Glenda Lappan

James T. Fey

William M. Fitzgerald

Susan N. Friel

Elizabeth Difanis Phillips

Boston, Massachusetts · Glenview, Illinois · Shoreview, Minnesota · Upper Saddle River, New Jersey

Connected Mathematics™ was developed at Michigan State University with financial support from the Michigan State University Office of the Provost, Computing and Technology, and the College of Natural Science.

This material is based upon work supported by the National Science Foundation under Grant No. MDR 9150217 and Grant No. ESI 9986372. Opinions expressed are those of the authors and not necessarily those of the Foundation.

The Michigan State University authors and administration have agreed that all MSU royalties arising from this publication will be devoted to purposes supported by the MSU Mathematics Education Enrichment Fund.

13-digit ISBN 978-0-13-366145-3
10-digit ISBN 0-13-366145-8
8 9 10 11 12 V003 15 14 13 12

Authors of Connected Mathematics

(from left to right) Glenda Lappan, Betty Phillips, Susan Friel, Bill Fitzgerald, Jim Fey

Glenda Lappan is a University Distinguished Professor in the Department of Mathematics at Michigan State University. Her research and development interests are in the connected areas of students' learning of mathematics and mathematics teachers' professional growth and change related to the development and enactment of K–12 curriculum materials.

James T. Fey is a Professor of Curriculum and Instruction and Mathematics at the University of Maryland. His consistent professional interest has been development and research focused on curriculum materials that engage middle and high school students in problem-based collaborative investigations of mathematical ideas and their applications.

William M. Fitzgerald *(Deceased)* was a Professor in the Department of Mathematics at Michigan State University. His early research was on the use of concrete materials in supporting student learning and led to the development of teaching materials for laboratory environments. Later he helped develop a teaching model to support student experimentation with mathematics.

Susan N. Friel is a Professor of Mathematics Education in the School of Education at the University of North Carolina at Chapel Hill. Her research interests focus on statistics education for middle-grade students and, more broadly, on teachers' professional development and growth in teaching mathematics K–8.

Elizabeth Difanis Phillips is a Senior Academic Specialist in the Mathematics Department of Michigan State University. She is interested in teaching and learning mathematics for both teachers and students. These interests have led to curriculum and professional development projects at the middle school and high school levels, as well as projects related to the teaching and learning of algebra across the grades.

Field Test Sites for CMP2

During the development of the revised edition of *Connected Mathematics* (CMP2), more than 100 classroom teachers have field-tested materials at 49 school sites in 12 states and the District of Columbia. This classroom testing occurred over three academic years (2001 through 2004), allowing careful study of the effectiveness of each of the 24 units that comprise the program. A special thanks to the students and teachers at these pilot schools.

Arkansas
Magnolia Public Schools
Kittena Bell*, Judith Trowell*; *Central Elementary School:* Maxine Broom, Betty Eddy, Tiffany Fallin, Bonnie Flurry, Carolyn Monk, Elizabeth Tye; *Magnolia Junior High School:* Monique Bryan, Ginger Cook, David Graham, Shelby Lamkin

Colorado
Boulder Public Schools
Nevin Platt Middle School: Judith Koenig
St. Vrain Valley School District, Longmont
Westview Middle School: Colleen Beyer, Kitty Canupp, Ellie Decker*, Peggy McCarthy, Tanya deNobrega, Cindy Payne, Ericka Pilon, Andrew Roberts

District of Columbia
Capitol Hill Day School: Ann Lawrence

Georgia
University of Georgia, Athens
Brad Findell
Madison Public Schools
Morgan County Middle School: Renee Burgdorf, Lynn Harris, Nancy Kurtz, Carolyn Stewart

Maine
Falmouth Public Schools
Falmouth Middle School: Donna Erikson, Joyce Hebert, Paula Hodgkins, Rick Hogan, David Legere, Cynthia Martin, Barbara Stiles, Shawn Towle*

Michigan
Portland Public Schools
Portland Middle School: Mark Braun, Holly DeRosia, Kathy Dole*, Angie Foote, Teri Keusch, Tammi Wardwell
Traverse City Area Public Schools
Bertha Vos Elementary: Kristin Sak; *Central Grade School:* Michelle Clark; Jody Meyers; *Eastern Elementary:* Karrie Tufts; *Interlochen Elementary:* Mary McGee-Cullen; *Long Lake Elementary:* Julie Faulkner*, Charlie Maxbauer, Katherine Sleder; *Norris Elementary:* Hope Slanaker; *Oak Park Elementary:* Jessica Steed; *Traverse Heights Elementary:* Jennifer Wolfert; *Westwoods Elementary:* Nancy Conn; *Old Mission Peninsula School:* Deb Larimer; *Traverse City East Junior High:* Ivanka Berkshire, Ruthanne Kladder, Jan Palkowski, Jane Peterson, Mary Beth Schmitt; *Traverse City West Junior High:* Dan Fouch*, Ray Fouch
Sturgis Public Schools
Sturgis Middle School: Ellen Eisele

Minnesota
Burnsville School District 191
Hidden Valley Elementary: Stephanie Cin, Jane McDevitt
Hopkins School District 270
Alice Smith Elementary: Sandra Cowing, Kathleen Gustafson, Martha Mason, Scott Stillman; *Eisenhower Elementary:* Chad Bellig, Patrick Berger, Nancy Glades, Kye Johnson, Shane Wasserman, Victoria Wilson; *Gatewood Elementary:* Sarah Ham, Julie Kloos, Janine Pung, Larry Wade; *Glen Lake Elementary:* Jacqueline Cramer, Kathy Hering, Cecelia Morris, Robb Trenda; *Katherine Curren Elementary:* Diane Bancroft, Sue DeWit, John Wilson; *L. H. Tanglen Elementary:* Kevin Athmann, Lisa Becker, Mary LaBelle, Kathy Rezac, Roberta Severson; *Meadowbrook Elementary:* Jan Gauger, Hildy Shank, Jessica Zimmerman; *North Junior High:* Laurel Hahn, Kristin Lee, Jodi Markuson, Bruce Mestemacher, Laurel Miller, Bonnie Rinker, Jeannine Salzer, Sarah Shafer, Cam Stottler; *West Junior High:* Alicia Beebe, Kristie Earl, Nobu Fujii, Pam Georgetti, Susan Gilbert, Regina Nelson Johnson, Debra Lindstrom, Michele Luke*, Jon Sorenson
Minneapolis School District 1
Ann Sullivan K-8 School: Bronwyn Collins; Anne Bartel* (Curriculum and Instruction Office)
Wayzata School District 284
Central Middle School: Sarajane Myers, Dan Nielsen, Tanya Ravenholdt
White Bear Lake School District 624
Central Middle School: Amy Jorgenson, Michelle Reich, Brenda Sammon

New York
New York City Public Schools
IS 89: Yelena Aynbinder, Chi-Man Ng, Nina Rapaport, Joel Spengler, Phyllis Tam*, Brent Wyso; *Wagner Middle School:* Jason Appel, Intissar Fernandez, Yee Gee Get, Richard Goldstein, Irving Marcus, Sue Norton, Bernadita Owens, Jennifer Rehn*, Kevin Yuhas

---

* indicates a Field Test Site Coordinator

Ohio

Talawanda School District, Oxford
Talawanda Middle School: Teresa Abrams, Larry Brock, Heather Brosey, Julie Churchman, Monna Even, Karen Fitch, Bob George, Amanda Klee, Pat Meade, Sandy Montgomery, Barbara Sherman, Lauren Steidl

Miami University
Jeffrey Wanko*

Springfield Public Schools
Rockway School: Jim Mamer

Pennsylvania

Pittsburgh Public Schools
Kenneth Labuskes, Marianne O'Connor, Mary Lynn Raith*; *Arthur J. Rooney Middle School:* David Hairston, Stamatina Mousetis, Alfredo Zangaro; *Frick International Studies Academy:* Suzanne Berry, Janet Falkowski, Constance Finseth, Romika Hodge, Frank Machi; *Reizenstein Middle School:* Jeff Baldwin, James Brautigam, Lorena Burnett, Glen Cobbett, Michael Jordan, Margaret Lazur, Melissa Munnell, Holly Neely, Ingrid Reed, Dennis Reft

Texas

Austin Independent School District
Bedichek Middle School: Lisa Brown, Jennifer Glasscock, Vicki Massey

El Paso Independent School District
Cordova Middle School: Armando Aguirre, Anneliesa Durkes, Sylvia Guzman, Pat Holguin*, William Holguin, Nancy Nava, Laura Orozco, Michelle Peña, Roberta Rosen, Patsy Smith, Jeremy Wolf

Plano Independent School District
Patt Henry, James Wohlgehagen*; *Frankford Middle School:* Mandy Baker, Cheryl Butsch, Amy Dudley, Betsy Eshelman, Janet Greene, Cort Haynes, Kathy Letchworth, Kay Marshall, Kelly McCants, Amy Reck, Judy Scott, Syndy Snyder, Lisa Wang; *Wilson Middle School:* Darcie Bane, Amanda Bedenko, Whitney Evans, Tonelli Hatley, Sarah (Becky) Higgs, Kelly Johnston, Rebecca McElligott, Kay Neuse, Cheri Slocum, Kelli Straight

Washington

Evergreen School District
Shahala Middle School: Nicole Abrahamsen, Terry Coon*, Carey Doyle, Sheryl Drechsler, George Gemma, Gina Helland, Amy Hilario, Darla Lidyard, Sean McCarthy, Tilly Meyer, Willow Neuwelt, Todd Parsons, Brian Pederson, Stan Posey, Shawn Scott, Craig Sjoberg, Lynette Sundstrom, Charles Switzer, Luke Youngblood

Wisconsin

Beaver Dam Unified School District
Beaver Dam Middle School: Jim Braemer, Jeanne Frick, Jessica Greatens, Barbara Link, Dennis McCormick, Karen Michels, Nancy Nichols*, Nancy Palm, Shelly Stelsel, Susan Wiggins

---

* indicates a Field Test Site Coordinator

Reviews of CMP to Guide Development of CMP2

Before writing for CMP2 began or field tests were conducted, the first edition of *Connected Mathematics* was submitted to the mathematics faculties of school districts from many parts of the country and to 80 individual reviewers for extensive comments.

School District Survey Reviews of CMP

Arizona
Madison School District #38 (Phoenix)

Arkansas
Cabot School District, Little Rock School District, Magnolia School District

California
Los Angeles Unified School District

Colorado
St. Vrain Valley School District (Longmont)

Florida
Leon County Schools (Tallahassee)

Illinois
School District #21 (Wheeling)

Indiana
Joseph L. Block Junior High (East Chicago)

Kentucky
Fayette County Public Schools (Lexington)

Maine
Selection of Schools

Massachusetts
Selection of Schools

Michigan
Sparta Area Schools

Minnesota
Hopkins School District

Texas
Austin Independent School District, The El Paso Collaborative for Academic Excellence, Plano Independent School District

Wisconsin
Platteville Middle School

Individual Reviewers of CMP

Arkansas

Deborah Cramer; Robby Frizzell *(Taylor)*; Lowell Lynde *(University of Arkansas, Monticello)*; Leigh Manzer *(Norfork)*; Lynne Roberts *(Emerson High School, Emerson)*; Tony Timms *(Cabot Public Schools)*; Judith Trowell *(Arkansas Department of Higher Education)*

California

José Alcantar *(Gilroy)*; Eugenie Belcher *(Gilroy)*; Marian Pasternack *(Lowman M. S. T. Center, North Hollywood)*; Susana Pezoa *(San Jose)*; Todd Rabusin *(Hollister)*; Margaret Siegfried *(Ocala Middle School, San Jose)*; Polly Underwood *(Ocala Middle School, San Jose)*

Colorado

Janeane Golliher *(St. Vrain Valley School District, Longmont)*; Judith Koenig *(Nevin Platt Middle School, Boulder)*

Florida

Paige Loggins *(Swift Creek Middle School, Tallahassee)*

Illinois

Jan Robinson *(School District #21, Wheeling)*

Indiana

Frances Jackson *(Joseph L. Block Junior High, East Chicago)*

Kentucky

Natalee Feese *(Fayette County Public Schools, Lexington)*

Maine

Betsy Berry *(Maine Math & Science Alliance, Augusta)*

Maryland

Joseph Gagnon *(University of Maryland, College Park)*; Paula Maccini *(University of Maryland, College Park)*

Massachusetts

George Cobb *(Mt. Holyoke College, South Hadley)*; Cliff Kanold *(University of Massachusetts, Amherst)*

Michigan

Mary Bouck *(Farwell Area Schools)*; Carol Dorer *(Slauson Middle School, Ann Arbor)*; Carrie Heaney *(Forsythe Middle School, Ann Arbor)*; Ellen Hopkins *(Clague Middle School, Ann Arbor)*; Teri Keusch *(Portland Middle School, Portland)*; Valerie Mills *(Oakland Schools, Waterford)*; Mary Beth Schmitt *(Traverse City East Junior High, Traverse City)*; Jack Smith *(Michigan State University, East Lansing)*; Rebecca Spencer *(Sparta Middle School, Sparta)*; Ann Marie Nicoll Turner *(Tappan Middle School, Ann Arbor)*; Scott Turner *(Scarlett Middle School, Ann Arbor)*

Minnesota

Margarita Alvarez *(Olson Middle School, Minneapolis)*; Jane Amundson *(Nicollet Junior High, Burnsville)*; Anne Bartel *(Minneapolis Public Schools)*; Gwen Ranzau Campbell *(Sunrise Park Middle School, White Bear Lake)*; Stephanie Cin *(Hidden Valley Elementary, Burnsville)*; Joan Garfield *(University of Minnesota, Minneapolis)*; Gretchen Hall *(Richfield Middle School, Richfield)*; Jennifer Larson *(Olson Middle School, Minneapolis)*; Michele Luke *(West Junior High, Minnetonka)*; Jeni Meyer *(Richfield Junior High, Richfield)*; Judy Pfingsten *(Inver Grove Heights Middle School, Inver Grove Heights)*; Sarah Shafer *(North Junior High, Minnetonka)*; Genni Steele *(Central Middle School, White Bear Lake)*; Victoria Wilson *(Eisenhower Elementary, Hopkins)*; Paul Zorn *(St. Olaf College, Northfield)*

New York

Debra Altenau-Bartolino *(Greenwich Village Middle School, New York)*; Doug Clements *(University of Buffalo)*; Francis Curcio *(New York University, New York)*; Christine Dorosh *(Clinton School for Writers, Brooklyn)*; Jennifer Rehn *(East Side Middle School, New York)*; Phyllis Tam *(IS 89 Lab School, New York)*;

Marie Turini *(Louis Armstrong Middle School, New York)*; Lucy West *(Community School District 2, New York)*; Monica Witt *(Simon Baruch Intermediate School 104, New York)*

Pennsylvania

Robert Aglietti *(Pittsburgh)*; Sharon Mihalich *(Pittsburgh)*; Jennifer Plumb *(South Hills Middle School, Pittsburgh)*; Mary Lynn Raith *(Pittsburgh Public Schools)*

Texas

Michelle Bittick *(Austin Independent School District)*; Margaret Cregg *(Plano Independent School District)*; Sheila Cunningham *(Klein Independent School District)*; Judy Hill *(Austin Independent School District)*; Patricia Holguin *(El Paso Independent School District)*; Bonnie McNemar *(Arlington)*; Kay Neuse *(Plano Independent School District)*; Joyce Polanco *(Austin Independent School District)*; Marge Ramirez *(University of Texas at El Paso)*; Pat Rossman *(Baker Campus, Austin)*; Cindy Schimek *(Houston)*; Cynthia Schneider *(Charles A. Dana Center, University of Texas at Austin)*; Uri Treisman *(Charles A. Dana Center, University of Texas at Austin)*; Jacqueline Weilmuenster *(Grapevine-Colleyville Independent School District)*; LuAnn Weynand *(San Antonio)*; Carmen Whitman *(Austin Independent School District)*; James Wohlgehagen *(Plano Independent School District)*

Washington

Ramesh Gangolli *(University of Washington, Seattle)*

Wisconsin

Susan Lamon *(Marquette University, Hales Corner)*; Steve Reinhart *(retired, Chippewa Falls Middle School, Eau Claire)*

Table of Contents

Data Distributions
Describing Variability and Comparing Groups

Unit Opener 2

Mathematical Highlights 4

Investigation 1 — Making Sense of Variability 5

1.1 Variability in Categorical Data 6

1.2 Variability in Numerical Counts 9

1.3 Variability in Numerical Measurements 12

1.4 Two Kinds of Variability 13

ACE Homework 16

Mathematical Reflections 27

Investigation 2 — Making Sense of Measures of Center 28

2.1 The Mean as an Equal Share 29

2.2 The Mean as a Balance Point in a Distribution 32

2.3 Repeated Values in a Distribution 36

2.4 Median and Mean and Shapes of Distributions 40

ACE Homework 44

Mathematical Reflections 54

Investigation 3   **Comparing Distributions:**
Equal Numbers of Data Values 55

3.1 **Measuring and Describing Reaction Times** 55

3.2 **Comparing Reaction Times** 57

3.3 **Comparing More Than a Few Students:**
Comparing Many Data Values 60

3.4 **Comparing Fastest and Slowest Trials:**
Comparing Larger Distributions 61

ACE **Homework** 62

Mathematical Reflections 73

Investigation 4   **Comparing Distributions:**
Unequal Numbers of Data Values 74

4.1 **Representing Survey Data** 74

4.2 **Are Steel Coasters Faster Than Wood Coasters?:**
Comparing Speed 76

ACE **Homework** 78

Mathematical Reflections 85

Looking Back and Looking Ahead 86

English/Spanish Glossary 89

Academic Vocabulary 94

Reaction Time Cards 96

Index 103

Acknowledgments 105

Data Distributions

Describing Variability and Comparing Groups

Is the proportion of each of the colors of jellybeans in a bag always the same?

In a graph displaying the kinds of pets that students have, there are several *repeated values*, such as "cat," "dog," "fish," and "rabbit." For other data, such as "pig," there are no repeated values. What do you think a repeated value means when we talk about data?

Willa, a video-game designer, needs an idea about how much time to give a player to react when an object appears on the screen. How can she use data from a reaction-time experiment to help her?

Statistics and data analysis are used to report health risks, to summarize consumer choices for CD players, to identify the most popular movies watched over a weekend, and to indicate favorite food choices. Think for a minute about some other ways statistics and graphs are used to report information.

There are important ideas about data analysis and statistics that can help you understand, analyze, critique, and respond to various reports that you encounter. Understanding data analysis and statistics can help you decide whether information is reliable or is distorted by the graphs used to display it. The investigations in *Data Distributions* will help you use ideas about statistics and data analysis to describe the variability in a data set, to compare groups, and to make decisions as you solve problems. Think about some interesting situations that involve statistical investigations, including the three on the previous page.

Mathematical Highlights

Describing Variability and Comparing Groups

In *Data Distributions*, you will explore important ideas related to statistics and data analysis, especially those related to describing variability and center and to making comparisons.

You will learn how to

- Apply the process of statistical investigation to pose questions, to identify ways data are collected, and to determine strategies for analyzing data in order to answer the questions posed

- Recognize that variability occurs whenever data are collected and describe the variability in the distribution of a given data set

- Identify sources of variability, including natural variability and variability that results from errors in measurement

- Determine whether to use the mean or median to describe a distribution

- Use the shape of a distribution to estimate the location of the mean and the median

- Use a variety of representations, including tables, bar graphs, and line plots, to display distributions

- Understand and use counts or percents to report frequencies of occurrence of data

- Compare the distributions of data sets using their related centers, variability, and shapes

- Decide if a difference among data values or summary measures matters

- Develop and use strategies to compare data sets to solve problems

As you work on problems in this unit, ask yourself questions about situations that involve analyzing distributions or comparing groups:

Is there anything surprising about the data and their distribution?

Where do the data cluster in the distribution?

How can I use the mean or median and range to help me understand and describe a data distribution?

What strategies can I use to compare two different data sets?

Making Sense of Variability

A statistical investigation begins with a question. Decisions about what data to collect are based on the question that is asked.

When data are collected to answer a question, the data may be similar to each other, such as the number of raisins found in each of 30 different half-ounce boxes of raisins. More often, however, the data are different from each other, such as pulse rates collected from 30 different people after each person rides a roller coaster.

Variability of a set of numerical data indicates how widely spread or closely clustered the data values are.

For each situation below, do you expect the data to be more similar to or different from each other? Why?

Each student records the number of each color of jellybeans found in his or her own bag.

Each student measures the same student's head size in centimeters.

Each student collects his or her reaction times on five trials using a computer reaction-time game.

Each student records his or her grade level—sixth grade, seventh grade, or eighth grade—as part of the data collected on a school survey.

1.1 Variability in Categorical Data

Data that are specific labels or names for categories are called **categorical data.** Suppose you ask people in which months they were born or what their favorite rock groups are. Their answers are categorical data. When displaying categorical data using tables or graphs, you usually report the *frequency*, or "how many," of each category in the data set as a count or a percent.

Last June, Jellybean Barn changed the packaging of their popular snack size Barn Mix from a blue bag to a green bag. Did Jellybean Barn plan a specific distribution of colors of jellybeans before June?

- What kinds of data would help answer the question?
- How might you collect such data?
- How would you analyze the data?
- How would you use your analysis to help answer the question?

One student uses a database that gives data for 200 pre-June bags of jellybeans. The database shows how many of each color jellybean were in each of the 200 bags. She uses the counts from the first bag to make a bar graph that shows the *percent* of each color of jellybean in the bag.

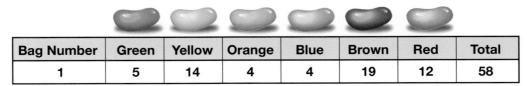

Bag Number	Green	Yellow	Orange	Blue	Brown	Red	Total
1	5	14	4	4	19	12	58

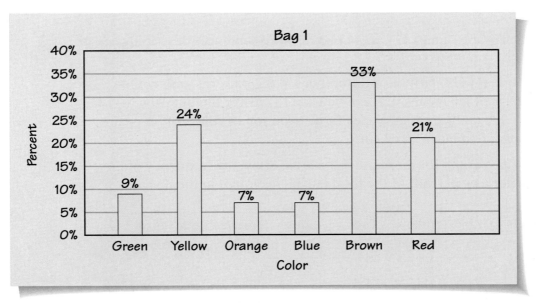

How did the student use the counts of the data to graph the percents?

The student noticed that the percent varied considerably from color to color.

There were more yellow, brown, and red jellybeans than green, orange, and blue jellybeans.

Brown jellybeans took up the greatest percentage of the bag; $\frac{1}{3}$, or about 33%, of the bag of jellybeans was brown.

The yellow and the red jellybeans were close in quantity, with yellow a little less than $\frac{1}{4}$, or 25%, of the bag and red a little more than $\frac{1}{5}$, or 20%, of the bag.

The green, orange, and blue jellybeans were each less than $\frac{1}{10}$, or 10%, of the bag.

A. 1. The table shows data from two other bags of jellybeans. Make a bar graph for each set of data. Show the frequency of each color as a percent of the total jellybeans in that bag.

Bag Number	Green	Yellow	Orange	Blue	Brown	Red	Total
2	5	15	2	7	15	10	54
3	3	13	5	5	19	10	55

2. For each graph in part (1), write two or more sentences describing the data.

3. Are there any similarities or differences in the patterns among the three bags of jellybeans that can be used to answer the question, "Did Jellybean Barn plan a specific distribution of colors of pre-June jellybeans?" Explain.

B. 1. Make a bar graph for these pre-June data. Show the frequency of each color as a percent of the total jellybeans found in the 30 bags.

Bag Number	Green	Yellow	Orange	Blue	Brown	Red	Total
1–30	92	449	109	90	576	415	1,731

2. Write two or more sentences describing the data in the bar graph.

3. How would you now answer the question, "Did Jellybean Barn plan a specific distribution of colors of pre-June jellybeans?"

C. Look at the eight graphs on the next page. Did Jellybean Barn make a change in the distribution of colors last June? If so, describe the change. Explain your reasoning.

ACE **Homework starts on page 17.**

1.2 Variability in Numerical Counts

Data that are counts or measures are called **numerical data.** We often count to gather numerical data. For example, we count people to find the population of each state in the United States in order to answer the question, "How much do state populations vary in size?"

Before June

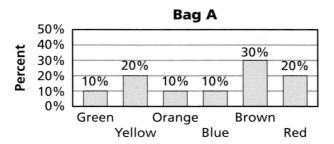

Bag A

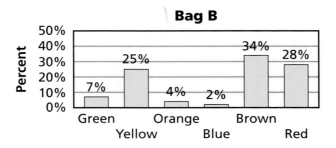

Bag B

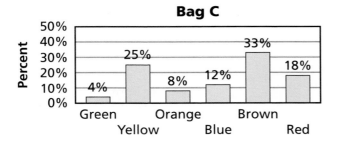

Bag C

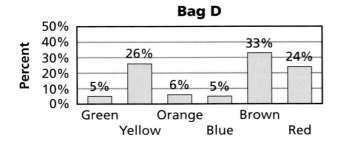

Bag D

After June

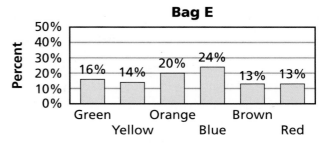

Bag E

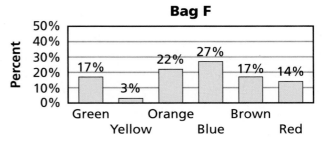

Bag F

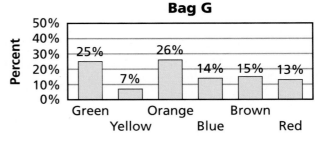

Bag G

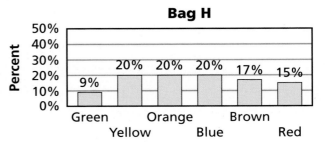

Bag H

Use the table and related graphs to answer the questions in Problem 1.2.

Immigration to the United States

Decade	Immigrants From Europe (Graph 1)	Total Immigrants	Percent of Immigrants From Europe (Graph 2)
1820	7,650	8,385	82%
1821–1830	98,797	143,439	69%
1831–1840	495,681	599,125	83%
1841–1850	1,597,442	1,713,251	93%
1851–1860	2,452,577	2,598,214	94%
1861–1870	2,064,141	2,314,824	89%
1871–1880	2,271,925	2,812,191	81%
1881–1890	4,735,484	5,246,613	90%
1891–1900	3,555,352	3,687,564	96%
1901–1910	8,056,040	8,795,386	92%
1911–1920	4,321,887	5,735,811	75%
1921–1930	2,463,194	4,107,209	60%
1931–1940	347,566	528,431	66%
1941–1950	621,147	1,035,039	60%
1951–1960	1,325,727	2,515,479	53%
1961–1970	1,123,492	3,321,677	34%
1971–1980	800,368	4,493,314	18%
1981–1990	761,550	7,338,062	10%
1991–2000	1,359,737	9,095,417	15%

SOURCE: U.S. Citizenship and Immigration Services. Go to www.PHSchool.com for a data update.
Web Code: ang-9041

Graph 1: Immigration From Europe to the United States

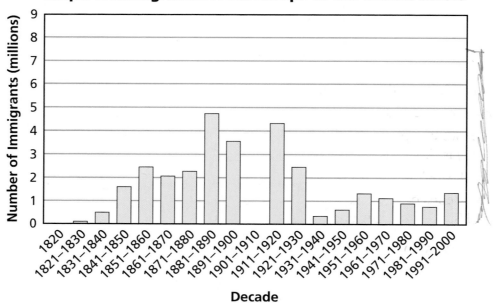

Graph 2: Immigration From Europe to the United States

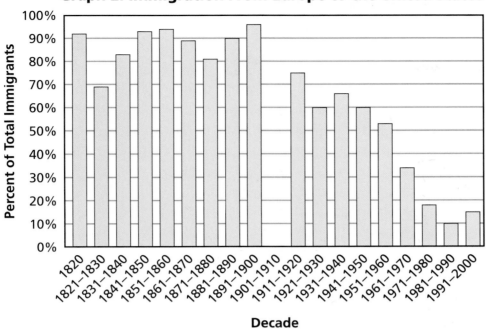

How did immigration from Europe to the United States change from 1820 to 2000?

Problem 1.2 Variability in Numerical Counts

A. 1. a. In the decade from 1901 to 1910, how many immigrants came from Europe? ⊘ *8,795,386*

b. Copy Graph 1 and add the bar for 1901–1910.

c. Write two comparison statements about how the 1901–1910 data value is similar to or different from the values for other decades. *Increase # of people about 4% less came from*

2. a. In the decade from 1901 to 1910, how many immigrants came from all countries? *8795386*

b. What percent of this number were immigrants from Europe? *92%*

c. Copy Graph 2 and add the bar for 1901–1910.

d. Write two comparison statements about how the percent in part (b) is similar to or different from the percents for other decades. *less from previous decades more then next decade*

B. Describe any trends or patterns you notice in immigration to the United States from Europe from 1820 to 2000. *Started high went down, went up, went up, up down, down up up down ....*

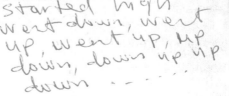

ACE Homework starts on page 17.

1.3 Variability in Numerical Measurements

Measurements, such as the time to run a mile or the height of a student, are another kind of numerical data. You already know that any measurement is approximate.

The measurement tools we use to gather data affect the precision of the measures we obtain. For example, one scale measures mass to the nearest tenth of a gram while another scale measures mass to the nearest thousandth of a gram. Also, when different people measure the same object, the results may differ even when they use the same tool.

What tool(s) might you use to measure heads in order to determine sizes needed for fitted baseball caps?

Problem 1.3 Variability in Numerical Measurements

Suppose your class wants to order fitted baseball caps with the *Mugwump* as a logo.

A. 1. Your teacher will choose one boy and one girl from the class to represent two different head sizes. Measure these two students' head sizes to the nearest tenth of a centimeter and record the data.

   2. Measure your own head size to the nearest tenth of a centimeter and record the data.

B. Use the data gathered by your class for Question A. Make a line plot for each of the following:

   1. the head-size measurements for the girl chosen

   2. the head-size measurements for the boy chosen

   3. the head-size measurements of all the students in the class

C. For each line plot in Question B:

   1. What are the minimum and maximum values of the distribution?

   2. What is the range of the distribution?

   3. Do you think the range of the measurements is great enough that recommending a single cap size would be difficult? Explain.

   4. Are there any unusually high or low data values, or *outliers*? If so, what are they?

   5. Do some or most of the data cluster in one or more locations? If so, where does this occur?

   6. Are there gaps in the data? If so, where do they occur?

7. What would you describe as a typical head size for these data? Explain.

8. Use these ideas to describe the variability in the data.

 ACE Homework starts on page 17.

1.4 Two Kinds of Variability

Each of 13 students measured the circumference of Jasmine's head. The results are shown using a table and a graph called a **value bar graph.**

Head Measurements

Name	Measure (cm)
Santo	56.0
Sara	55.8
Pam	56.0
Melosa	55.9
Malik	55.5
Martin	56.0
Ming	55.2
Manny	56.5
Juanita	55.0
Jun	55.5
Tai	56.0
Kareem	55.5
Chip	55.8

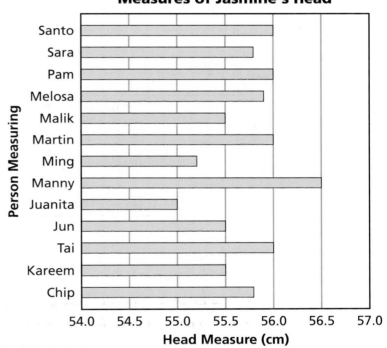

Measures of Jasmine's Head

How are the table and the value bar graph related?

What is a value bar graph?

The variability results from measurement errors as different students measured the circumference of Jasmine's head.

How do you think measurement errors occur?

The **ordered value bar graph** shows the data in order from minimum to maximum values.

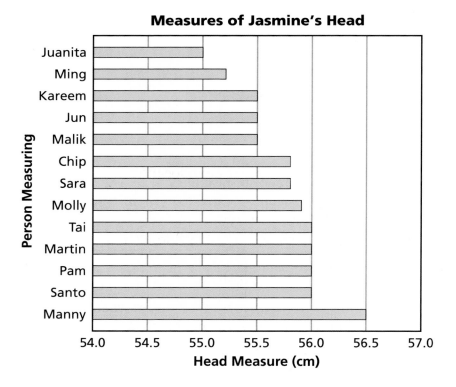

The **line plots** show the frequency of each measurement.

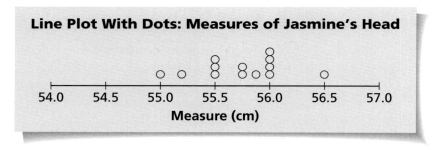

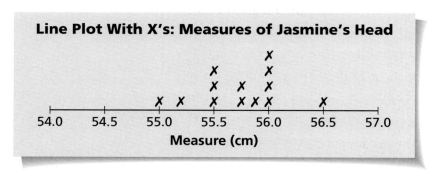

How are the ordered value bar graph and the line plots related?

What does each graph tell you about the distribution of these data?

Use the ordered value bar graph and the line plots on the facing page.

A. 1. Examine the distribution of the measurements. What are the minimum and maximum values?

   2. What is the range?

   3. Is the range of the measurements great enough that choosing a cap size for Jasmine would be difficult? Explain.

   4. Are there any outliers? If so, what are they?

   5. Do some or most of the data cluster in one or more locations? Explain.

   6. Are there gaps in the data? If so, where do they occur?

   7. What measurement would you recommend using to choose a cap size for Jasmine? Explain.

   8. Use these ideas to describe the variability in the data set.

B. 1. Jasmine's classmates measured their own head sizes and recorded them in the table below. Make an ordered value bar graph and a line plot for these data.

Class Head Sizes

Initials	CK	KN	TB	JG	JW	MD	MG
Measure (cm)	55.8	58.0	56.5	58.0	55.5	58.0	55.2

Initials	MJ	MR	MS	PM	SF	SK
Measure (cm)	58.5	55.2	55.5	54.0	57.0	56.4

   2. What are the minimum and maximum values?

   3. What is the range?

   4. Is the range of the measurements great enough that recommending one cap size for all the students would be difficult? Explain.

   5. Are there any outliers? If so, what are they?

   6. Do some or most of the data cluster in one or more locations? Explain.

   7. Are there gaps in the data? If so, where do they occur?

   8. What would you describe as the typical cap size for these students? Explain.

   9. Use these ideas to describe the variability in the data set.

ACE Homework starts on page 17.

Applications

1. a. Use the jellybean data for Bag 1, Bag 2, and Bag 3. For each bag, make a bar graph that shows the percent of each color found.

Jellybean Colors

Bag Number	Green	Yellow	Orange	Blue	Brown	Red	Total
1	3	10	9	5	10	18	55
2	5	12	4	6	19	11	57
3	7	10	9	4	16	12	58
4	4	14	2	1	14	19	54
5	12	7	8	7	14	13	61
6	10	9	6	5	15	8	53
7	11	11	6	6	12	12	58
8	8	15	5	3	16	10	57
9	2	11	4	4	24	12	57
10	5	7	4	1	26	13	56
11	6	13	4	4	15	18	60
12	5	8	4	2	23	16	58
13	9	13	4	4	14	11	55
14	9	10	5	5	14	14	57
15	5	19	5	2	13	14	58
Total	101	169	79	59	245	201	854

b. Write two or more comparison statements that describe the distribution of colors for the three bags.

c. Is there some plan to the distribution of colors in the bags? Explain.

2. a. Use the totals in the last row of the table for each color of jellybeans. Make a bar graph for these data that shows the percent of each color found in the 15 bags.

b. Describe the data by writing two or more comparison statements.

c. Look back at the bar graph you made for Problem 1.1, Question B. Compare this graph with the graph you made in part (a). How would you now answer the question, "Did Jellybean Barn plan a specific distribution of colors of pre-June jellybeans?" Explain.

3. a. The line plot below shows the head measurements of several seventh-grade students. What are the minimum and maximum values?

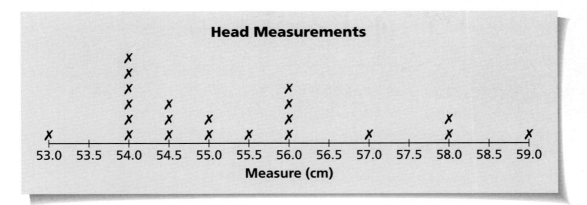

Head Measurements

Measure (cm)

b. What is the range?

c. Is the range of the measurements great enough that recommending one cap size for all the students would be difficult? Explain.

d. Are there any outliers? If so, what are they?

e. Do some or most of the data cluster in one or more locations? If so, where?

f. Are there gaps in the data? If so, where do they occur?

g. What would you describe as the typical cap size for these students?

h. How might you use these ideas to describe the variability in the data?

For each situation in Exercises 4–7, tell whether the data collected are categorical or numerical. Then, tell whether the data are widely spread out or closely clustered.

4. Each student records the number of people living in his or her household.

5. Each student measures the length of the same table in centimeters.

6. Each student randomly chooses a number from 1 to 10.

7. Each student records the time spent viewing television, videos, and DVD movies in the past week.

Homework
Help **Online**
PHSchool.com
For: Help with Exercises 4–7
Web Code: ane-8104

For Exercises 8–11, use the table below.

Immigration to the United States

Decade	Immigrants From Mexico	Total Immigrants	Percent of Immigrants From Mexico
1820	1	8,385	0%
1821–1830	4,817	143,439	3%
1831–1840	6,599	599,125	1%
1841–1850	3,271	1,713,251	0%
1851–1860	3,078	2,598,214	0%
1861–1870	2,191	2,314,824	0%
1871–1880	5,162	2,812,191	0%
1881–1890	1,913	5,246,613	0%
1891–1900	971	3,687,564	0%
1901–1910	49,642	8,795,386	1%
1911–1920	219,004	5,735,811	4%
1921–1930	459,287	4,107,209	11%
1931–1940	22,319	528,431	4%
1941–1950	60,589	1,035,039	6%
1951–1960	299,811	2,515,479	12%
1961–1970	453,937	3,321,677	14%
1971–1980	640,294	4,493,314	14%
1981–1990	1,655,843	7,338,062	23%
1991–2000	2,249,421	9,095,417	25%

SOURCE: U.S. Citizenship and Immigration Services. Go to www.PHSchool.com for a data update.
Web Code: ang-9041

8. **a.** In each of the decades 1961–1970 and 1971–1980, how many people were immigrants from Mexico?

   b. Copy the graph below. Add the bars for 1961–1970 and 1971–1980.

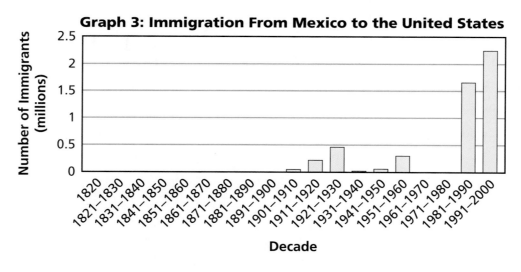

Graph 3: Immigration From Mexico to the United States

9. Multiple Choice Which statement is true?

A. More immigrants came to the United States in the decade 1941–1950 than in the decade 1961–1970.

B. About the same number of immigrants came to the United States in the decade 1921–1930 as in the decade 1961–1970.

C. The number of immigrants in the decade 1991–2000 is about 50,000 more than the combined number of immigrants for the two decades 1971–1990.

D. None of the above.

10. a. In each of the decades 1961–1970 and 1971–1980, how many people total were immigrants to the United States?

b. What percent of each of the numbers in part (a) were immigrants from Mexico?

c. Copy the graph below. Add the bars for 1961–1970 and 1971–1980.

Graph 4: Immigration From Mexico to the United States

d. Write two comparison statements about how the data values in part (c) are similar to or different from the data values for other decades.

11. How has the pattern of immigration from Mexico to the United States changed from 1820 to 2000? Explain.

12. a. One of the line plots below shows several measures of Yukio's head. The other shows one measure of Yukio's head and one of each of his classmates' heads. Identify the line plot that shows Yukio's head measurements. Explain your reasoning.

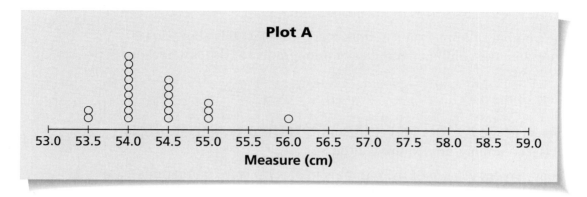

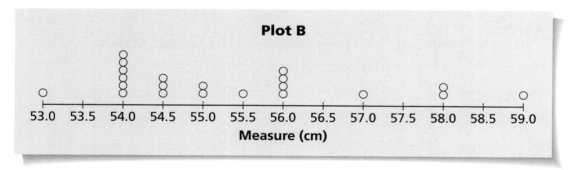

b. Identify the line plot that shows the head measurements of Yukio and his classmates.

13. a. The table below shows the data for the brown jellybeans from Bags 4–9 of Exercise 1. Make an ordered value bar graph and a line plot for these data.

Go Online
PHSchool.com

For: Multiple Choice Skills Practice
Web Code: ana-8154

Brown Jellybeans

Bag Number	4	5	6	7	8	9
Number of Brown Jellybeans	14	14	15	12	16	24

b. What are the minimum and maximum values?

c. What is the range?

d. Are there gaps or clusters of data? Explain.

e. Would an ordered value bar graph or a line plot better represent the data? Explain.

Connections

14. There are 100 jellybeans in Bag A. Given the following statements, how many jellybeans of each color are there?

- $\frac{3}{10}$ are brown
- 0.25 are yellow
- 0.1 are green

- $\frac{2}{10}$ are red
- the ratio of red jellybeans to blue jellybeans is 2 : 1
- 0.05 are orange

15. There are 80 jellybeans in Bag B. Given the following statements, how many jellybeans of each color are there?

- 30% are brown
- 0.25 are yellow
- the ratio of brown jellybeans to blue jellybeans is 3 : 1

- 20% are red
- 0.05 are green
- the ratio of orange jellybeans to green jellybeans is 2 : 1

16. Multiple Choice The stem-and-leaf plot shows the heights of a group of students. What percent of the students are more than 5 feet tall?

Student Heights

4	3 3 4 5 6 7 7 8 9
5	0 0 1 1 2 2 2 6 8 8 9
6	0 0 3 5 5

Key: 5 | 2 means 52 inches

F. 44% **G.** 20% **H.** 12% **J.** 80%

17. a. Describe any trends or patterns in immigration to the United States from Asia from 1820 to 2000 using the graph below.

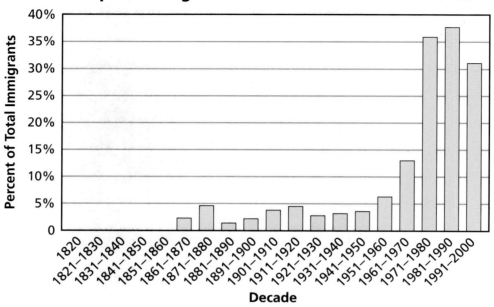

Graph 5: Immigration From Asia to the United States

Source: U.S. Citizenship and Immigration Services. Go to www.PHSchool.com for a data update. Web Code: ang-9041

b. Write two comparison statements about the trends in immigration from **Mexico** to the United States (Exercises 8–11) and from **Asia** to the United States from 1820 to 2000.

c. Look back at Graph 2 in Problem 1.2. As the trend for immigration from Europe was decreasing from 1961 to 2000, what happened to the trends for immigration from Mexico and Asia?

18. Multiple Choice Ms. Turini's math class took a test on Monday. The scores for the exam were: 98, 79, 65, 84, 87, 92, 90, 61, 93, 76, 72, and 93. Which stem-and-leaf plot correctly displays these data?

A.

6	| |
7	| | |
8	| |
9	＋＋＋＋＋

B.

6	1 5
7	2 6 9
8	4 7
9	0 2 3 3 8

C.

6	5 1
7	9 6 2
8	4 7
9	8 2 0 3 3

D.

6	1 5
7	2 6 9
8	4 7
9	2 3 3 8

19. a. The tables below show prices for skateboards at four different sporting goods stores. For each store, make a stem-and-leaf plot that will show the distribution of prices for skateboards from that store.

Store A	
$60	$50
$40	$50
$13	$60
$45	$50
$20	$25
$30	$15
$35	$70
$60	$120
$50	$90
$70	

Store B	
$13	$70
$40	$50
$45	$70
$60	$50
$50	$10
$30	$120
$15	$90
$35	$120
$15	

Store C	
$40	$50
$20	$60
$60	$70
$35	$70
$50	$50
$30	$90
$13	$120
$45	$120
$40	$200

Store D	
$179	$145
$160	$149
$149	$149
$149	$149
$149	$149
$145	$145
$149	$150
$100	$149
$179	$149

b. How do the prices for skateboards compare across the four stores? Write statements that make your reasoning clear.

c. Look at the four stem-and-leaf plots. What is the typical price for skateboards for each store? Explain your reasoning.

d. Describe the variability in the prices of skateboards.

20. Make a line plot to show the distribution of head-size measures that matches the criteria below.

● There are 10 data points.

● The measures vary from 54 cm to 57.5 cm.

● The mode is 55 cm; there are three data values at the mode.

● The median is 55.5 cm.

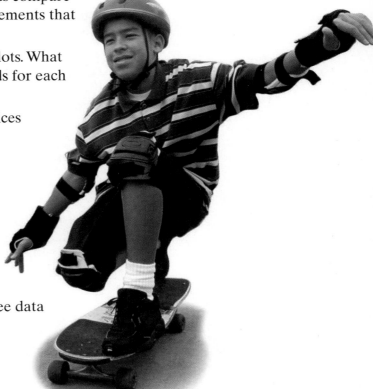

Extensions

For Exercise 21, use the data in the table below.

Presidential Fitness Test Standards

Tests	Time (seconds)			
	Age 11	Age 12	Age 13	Age 14
Boys—Shuttle Run	10.0	9.8	9.5	9.1
Girls—Shuttle Run	10.5	10.4	10.2	10.1
Boys—Mile Run	452	431	410	386
Girls—Mile Run	542	500	493	479

SOURCE: The President's Council on Physical Fitness and Sports

21. Each graph is marked with a reference line that shows the Presidential Fitness Standard Time for the age group.

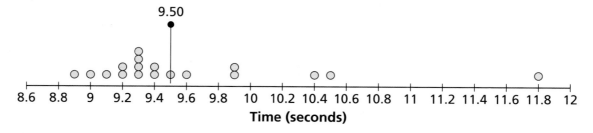

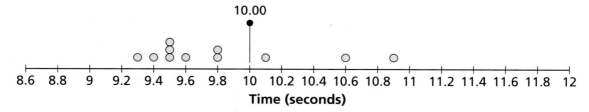

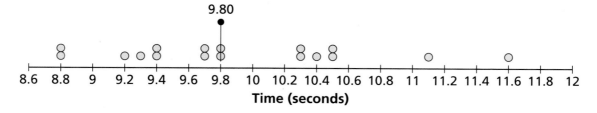

a. Estimate the minimum and maximum times in each distribution.

b. Estimate the range of each distribution.

c. Does the range seem "large" or "small" for each set of data? Explain your reasoning.

d. Are there any outliers? If so, what are they?

e. Do some or most of the data in each distribution cluster in one or more locations? If so, where?

f. Are there gaps in any set of data? If so, where do they occur?

g. How would you describe the typical shuttle run time for each age group of boys?

h. Describe the variability in each of the three distributions.

i. How do the fitness test results in each graph compare to the Presidential Standards for that age level? Explain.

22. **a.** Estimate the minimum and maximum shuttle run times shown in the scatter plot.

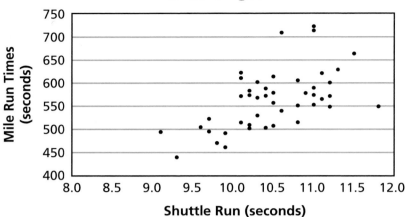

Shuttle Run and Mile Run Times for Girls Ages 11–13

b. Estimate the minimum and maximum mile run times.

c. Copy the scatter plot. Sketch the line $y = 50x$ where y is the time for the mile run and x is the time for the shuttle run.

d. What can you say about the times that are on this line? Times that are above this line? Times that are below this line?

e. Is there a relationship between Times for Mile Run and Times for Shuttle Run? Explain.

23. Multiple Choice Janelle makes a scatter plot that shows the relationship between the number of music downloads she has made and the amount of unused disk space she has left. Which statement is true?

F. As the number of music downloads increases, the amount of unused disk space increases.

G. As the number of music downloads increases, the amount of unused disk space stays the same.

H. As the number of music downloads decreases, the amount of unused disk space increases.

J. As the number of music downloads decreases, the amount of disk space used decreases.

Mathematical Reflections 1

In this investigation, you explored how data in a distribution vary. These questions will help you summarize what you have learned.

Think over your answers to these questions. Discuss your ideas with other students and your teacher. Then write a summary of your findings in your notebook.

1. Use the situation below to help you answer parts (a)–(e).

Students collected data from their classmates to answer each of these three questions:

- *What is the typical bedtime for students?*
- *What are students' favorite kinds of pets?*
- *What is the typical number of pets students have?*

a. What measures are used to describe variability?

b. Define the range of a distribution of data so a sixth-grader would understand.

c. How would you help a sixth-grade student understand the difference between categorical data and numerical data?

d. What does it mean when we say categorical data vary?

e. What does it mean when we say numerical data vary?

2. In which situations might you report frequencies of data using actual counts? In which might you use percents? How do you decide?

3. Describe how displaying data in tables or graphs can help you identify patterns or determine what is typical about a distribution.

Making Sense of Measures of Center

Statistics are numbers that are part of your everyday world. They are used in reporting on baseball, basketball, football, soccer, the Olympics, and other sports. Statistics are used to highlight the top hitters in baseball or top free-throw shooters in basketball. Identifying gold-medal skating champions depends on the statistics used to interpret scores from their performances during different events.

- What sports are these stats from? What do they mean?

    RBI   free-throw percentage
    ERA   yards per game

When you analyze data, the variability in a distribution is important. However, you also want to describe what is typical about a distribution. Three statistics that are often used to help describe what is typical about distributions are the *mean*, the *median*, and the *mode*.

Means, medians, and modes are called **measures of center.**

How is a measure of center influenced by the variability in a distribution of data?

There are other statistics you can use to describe variability. You can describe the distribution of data by its *range*. The **range** is the difference between the maximum and minimum values in a distribution. You can also give the minimum and maximum values to show how the data vary. You may notice unusual values and wonder if any of these data are **outliers.** Or you may notice that data with similar values form *clusters* in a distribution or that there are *gaps* with no data values.

2.1 The Mean as an Equal Share

The mean is one way to describe what is typical for a distribution. The **mean** is often called the "average" of the data. You can also think of the mean as the amount each person gets if everyone gets an equal share.

Getting Ready for Problem

Students are using beads for a class project. Marie has 5 beads, Sarah has 10 beads, Sri has 20 beads, and Jude has 25 beads. The students distribute their beads until everyone has the same number of beads. Each now has an equal share of the beads.

1. How many beads will each student have in the end?

2. How did you solve this problem?

When the redistributing is finished, each student has an equal share of the beads. This equal share of beads is the mean number of beads per person.

Marie's Beads

Sarah's Beads

Sri's Beads

Jude's Beads

Use the idea of mean as an equal share as you answer these questions.

A. Malaika has four 20-point projects in her science class.

1. The bar graph shows Malaika's scores on three of these projects. There is also a bar that shows Malaika's mean score for all four projects.

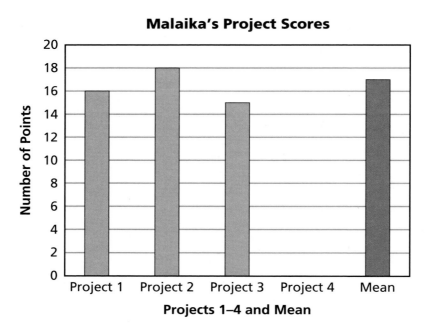

Malaika's Project Scores

a. Read the three project scores and the mean of the project scores. Use this information to find the number of points Malaika received on Project 4. Explain your reasoning.

b. What is the range of Malaika's scores on the four projects? What does this tell you about the variability of her scores?

2. a. When Malaika's total points for all four projects are distributed equally among the four projects, the result is 17 points per project, which is her mean score. Juan has a total of 60 points for the four projects. What is his mean score?

b. Give four possible project scores that would result in this mean score for Juan.

c. What is the range of Juan's scores on the four projects? Use the range to write a sentence about the variability of his scores.

d. Do Juan's scores vary more than Malaika's scores? Explain.

B. 1. a. On Monday, four servers receive the following amounts as tips while working at the Mugwump Diner. What is the range of the tips earned on Monday? What does this tell you about the variability of the tips?

Monday's Diner Tips

Server	Tip Amount
Maisha	$5.25
Brian	$4.75
Isabel	$6.50
Joe	$6.10

b. The four servers decide to share the tips equally. How much money per server is this?

2. Imala was forgotten when tips were shared. She received $6.10, the same amount that Joe originally received. Suppose Imala's tips are included with the others' tips and shared equally among the five servers. Would the first four servers receive less than, the same as, or more than they did before Imala's tips were included? Explain your reasoning.

3. a. On Tuesday, the five servers share their tips equally. The result is a mean of $6.45 per server. Does this tell you that one of the servers originally received $6.45 in tips? Why or why not?

b. What is a possible set of tips that would result in this mean?

4. a. On Wednesday, Isabel receives $3.40 in tips. When all of the tips are shared equally among the five servers, the result is $5.25 per server. Do you think this could happen? Explain.

b. Based on the information in part (a), what can you say about the range of tips earned on Wednesday? Explain.

ACE **Homework starts on page 44.**

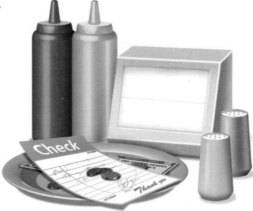

2.2 The Mean as a Balance Point in a Distribution

You can look at the mean as the balance point in a distribution. It acts like the fulcrum (FUL krum) for a seesaw. You can simulate this situation with a ruler, a cardboard tube (cut in half lengthwise), and some coins (all of the same type). The coins are placed along the board so that the board remains in balance on the cardboard tube. Look at the picture below for an example.

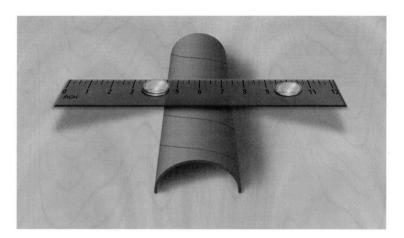

Notice that a coin placed far from the balance point can be balanced by a coin the same distance away on the other side of the balance point, by two coins half the distance away on the other side, or by three coins $\frac{1}{3}$ of the distance away on the other side.

The mean is a kind of fulcrum in a distribution of data. The data balance around the mean, much as the coins on the ruler balance around the fulcrum created by the tube.

The table below shows the number of calories and the amount of sugar per serving for nine cereals in the store.

Content Sugar of Cereals

Cereal	Calories	Sugar (g)
Cereal 1	90	5
Cereal 2	110	12
Cereal 3	220	8
Cereal 4	102	2
Cereal 5	120	6
Cereal 6	112	9
Cereal 7	107	12
Cereal 8	170	12
Cereal 9	121	6

Source: Bowes & Church's Food Values of Portions Commonly Used

You can make a line plot to show the distribution. The mean is 8 grams of sugar, the data vary from 2 to 12 grams of sugar, and the range is 10 grams of sugar. The distribution balances at 8 grams of sugar.

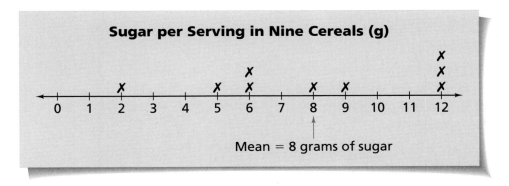

You can show this using a ruler and a cardboard tube. The ruler is marked with 13 main tick marks, one at 0 and one at each inch mark up to 12. Use nine coins of the same type. Place the ruler on the tube at the 8-inch mark, and place the coins along the ruler so they match the distribution shown above.

The Mean as a Balance Point in a Distribution

Use the idea of mean as a balance point as you answer these questions.

A. 1. There are nine cereals in a data set. The mean amount of sugar in the cereals is 6 grams per serving. One of the cereals has 10 grams of sugar in one serving. Make a line plot that shows a distribution of the amount of sugar. Then make a different line plot that meets the criteria. Explain how you designed each distribution.

   2. a. What is the range of each distribution you made?

   b. How do the ranges compare? Are they the same, or is one range greater than the other?

B. 1. Here is a set of data showing the amount of sugar in a serving for each of ten cereals, in grams:

   1   3   6   6   6   6   6   6   10   10

   a. Make a line plot to show this new distribution.

   b. What is the mean for these data?

   2. Make one or more changes to the data set in part (1) so that the mean is 7 and the range is:

   a. the same as the range of the original data set

   b. greater than the range of the original data set

   c. less than the range of the original data set

C. 1. Anica wonders if balancing the distribution has anything to do with how much the data values differ from the mean. She draws the diagram below. What is indicated by the arrows on each side of the line marking the mean?

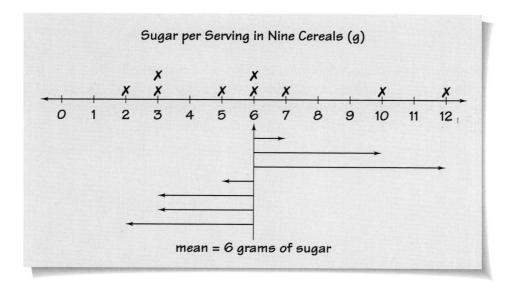

Sugar per Serving in Nine Cereals (g)

mean = 6 grams of sugar

2. Determine the length of each arrow. Find the sum of the lengths of the arrows on each side of the mean.

3. How do the two sums compare? Why do you think this is so?

4. Do you think this will always be true? Explain.

5. How might balancing the distribution relate to the distances of the data values from the mean? Explain.

D. Graph A and Graph B show two different distributions. Latoya guesses that each distribution has a mean of 5 grams of sugar per serving. For each distribution, answer parts (1)–(3).

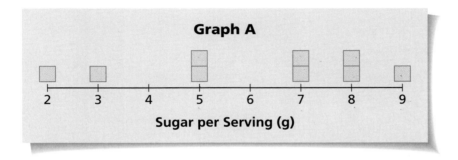

Graph A

Sugar per Serving (g)

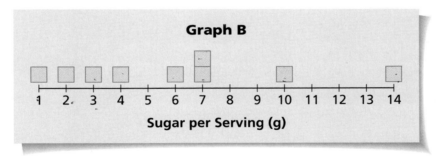

Graph B

Sugar per Serving (g)

1. Find the difference from Latoya's guess of 5 for each data value that is greater than 5. What is their sum?

2. Find the difference from Latoya's guess of 5 for each data value that is less than the mean. What is their sum?

3. Is Latoya correct that the mean is 5? Does the distribution "balance?" If so, explain. If not, change one or more of the values to make it balance.

ACE Homework starts on page 44.

Repeated Values in a Distribution

The graph below shows categorical data collected about the kinds of pets that 26 students have.

Pets Students Have

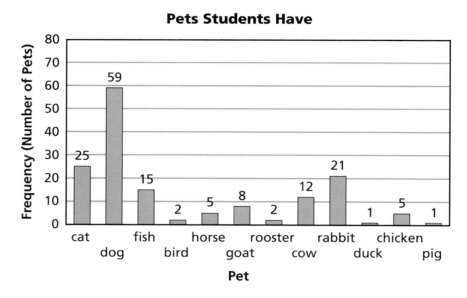

For "cat," "dog," "fish," and "rabbit," there are several *repeated values*. For other data, there are fewer repeated values. For both "duck" and "pig," there are no repeated values.

What do you think a repeated value means when we talk about data?

The **mode** is the data value that occurs most frequently in a set of data. For pets in this graph, the mode is "dog." When the data are categorical data, the mode is the only measure of center that can be used. It tells you the data value that is repeated the most often. For example, you can say that the mode kind of pet in the graph is a dog.

The **median** is the midpoint in an ordered distribution. In the graph of a distribution, data values are located below, above, or at this midpoint. The graph below shows numerical data about the numbers of pets each of the 26 students has.

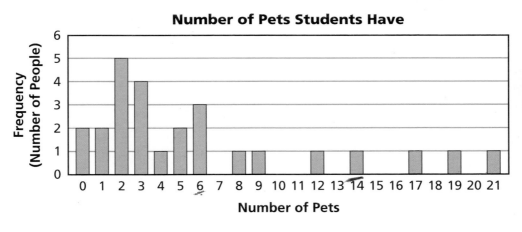

Number of Pets Students Have

Are there repeated values in this distribution?

Where would you mark the location of the median for these data?

Getting Ready for Problem 2.3

In Problem 2.2, you saw that the mean is like a fulcrum in a distribution. The data balance around the mean. Look at the graph above and consider these questions.

- What is the range of the data?
- What is the mean and where is it located?
- How does the location of the median compare to the location of the mean?
- Why do you think this is so?
- Do the data seem to cluster in some parts of the distribution?
- Does clustering of the data appear to be related to the locations of the median and the mean?

Problem 2.3 Repeated Values in a Distribution

A. Jorge is ordering pizza for a party. Tamika shows Jorge the graph at the right. She tells him to order only thin-crust pizzas because thin crust is the mode. Do you agree or disagree? Explain.

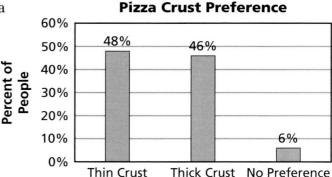

Pizza Crust Preference

B. The data from 70 cereals are shown below. Which option do you suggest using to find the typical amount of sugar in a serving of cereal? Explain.

Option 1 Use the mode, 3 grams. The typical amount of sugar in a serving of cereal is 3 grams.

Option 2 Use the median, 7.5 grams. The typical amount of sugar in a serving of cereal is 7.5 grams.

Option 3 Use clusters. There are several cereals that have either 3 or 6 grams of sugar per serving. 40% of the data seem to be evenly spread between 8 and 12 grams of sugar.

Option 4 Use something else. Write your own statement about what you consider to be the typical amount of sugar in a serving of cereal.

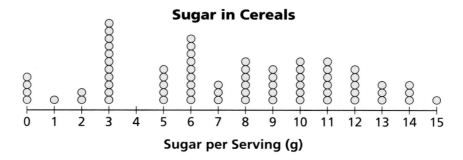

Sugar in Cereals

Sugar per Serving (g)

C. An advertiser wants more people to listen to a phone message. He uses the graph below.

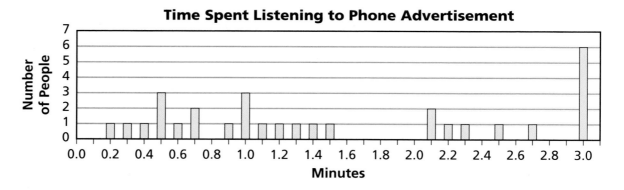

Time Spent Listening to Phone Advertisement

Minutes

Which of the options below should the advertiser use to decide how long the message should be? Explain.

Option 1 Use the mode. The most frequent amount of time spent listening to the phone advertisement was 3 minutes.

Option 2 Use the mean. Listening times lasted, on average, 1.51 minutes per person.

Option 3 Use clusters. One third of the people listened less than 1 minute and more than half listened less than 1.5 minutes. Only 20% of the people listened for 3 minutes.

Option 4 Use something else. Write your own response.

D. 1. In the plots below, the data for the 70 cereals in Question B are organized by the cereals' locations on the shelves in a supermarket. Use means, medians, clusters, or other strategies to compare the three distributions. Explain your reasoning.

2. Use the information from part (1) to make a prediction about the sugar content per serving of a cereal based on its shelf location.

Sugar in Top Shelf Cereals

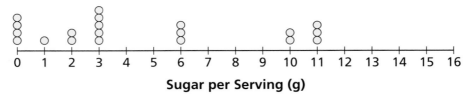

Sugar per Serving (g)

Sugar in Middle Shelf Cereals

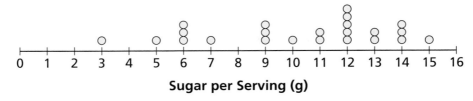

Sugar per Serving (g)

Sugar in Bottom Shelf Cereals

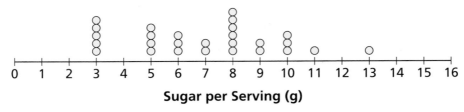

Sugar per Serving (g)

ACE Homework starts on page 44.

Unlike with categorical data, the mode is not always useful with numerical data. Sometimes there is no mode and sometimes there is more than one mode.

Sometimes the mean and median of a distribution are located close together. The graph below shows the distribution of the amount of sugar in cereals located on the bottom shelf in a supermarket. The mean and the median are marked. The median is 7 grams and the mean is 6.9 grams.

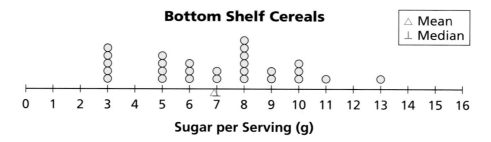

Bottom Shelf Cereals

△ Mean
⊥ Median

Sugar per Serving (g)

In some distributions the mean and median are located further apart. The graph below shows the distribution of the amount of sugar per serving in cereals on the top shelf in a supermarket. The mean and the median are marked. The median is 3 grams and the mean is 4.55 grams.

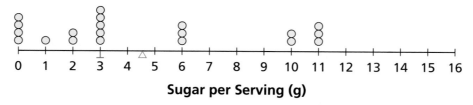

Sugar in Top Shelf Cereals

Sugar per Serving (g)

The overall shape of a distribution is determined by where the data cluster, where there are repeated values, and how spread out the data are. The shape of a distribution influences where the median and mean are located. In the next problem, you will experiment with making changes to distributions. Observe what these changes do to the locations of the mean and median in a distribution.

Problem 2.4 Measures of Center and Shapes of Distributions

For Questions A–C, predict what will happen. Then do the computation to see whether you are correct.

A. The graph below shows the distribution of the amount of sugar in 20 cereals found on the top shelf. The sum of the values in this distribution is 91 grams. Use stick-on notes to make a copy of the distribution. Note the location of the mean at 4.55 grams of sugar and the median at 3 grams of sugar.

Sugar in Top Shelf Cereals

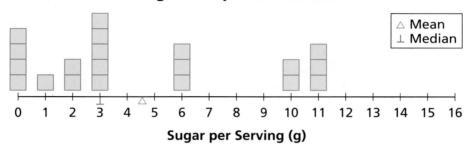

Sugar per Serving (g)

1. Suppose you remove the three cereals with 6 grams of sugar per serving and add three new cereals, each with 9 grams of sugar per serving. What happens to the mean and the median? Why do you think this happens?

2. **a.** Use the new distribution from part (1). Suppose you remove a cereal with 3 grams of sugar and add a cereal with 8 grams of sugar. How do the mean and the median change?

   b. Suppose you remove another cereal with 3 grams of sugar and add another cereal with 8 grams of sugar. How do the mean and the median change?

   c. Suppose you remove a third cereal with 3 grams of sugar and add a third cereal with 8 grams of sugar. How do the mean and the median change?

B. Use the new distribution from Question A, part (2). Experiment with removing data values and replacing them with new data values.

1. How does replacing smaller data values with larger data values affect the mean and the median?

2. How does replacing larger data values with smaller data values affect the mean and the median?

3. How does replacing larger and smaller data values with values that are closer to the middle of the distribution affect the mean and the median?

C. 1. Sort these eight distributions into two groups: one where the means and medians are the same or almost the same and one where they are not.

Sugar Distribution 1

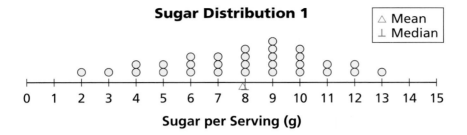

Sugar per Serving (g)

Sugar Distribution 2

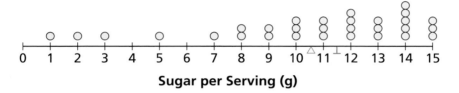

Sugar per Serving (g)

Sugar Distribution 3

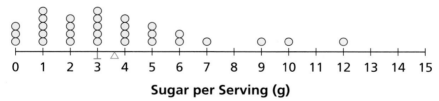

Sugar per Serving (g)

Sugar Distribution 4

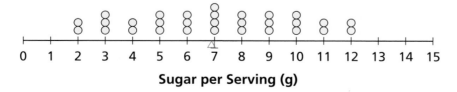

Sugar per Serving (g)

Sugar Distribution 5

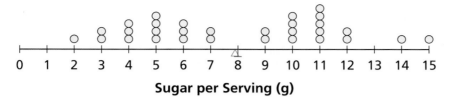

Sugar per Serving (g)

Sugar Distribution 6

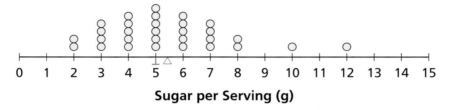

Sugar per Serving (g)

Sugar Distribution 7

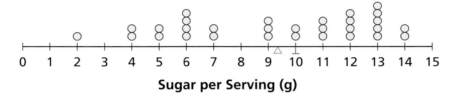

Sugar per Serving (g)

Sugar Distribution 8

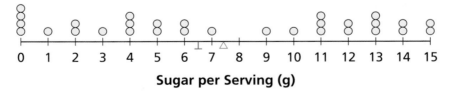

Sugar per Serving (g)

2. For each group of distributions, describe how the locations of the mean and median appear to be influenced by the shape of the distribution. Explain your reasoning.

ACE Homework starts on page 44.

Applications

1. a. Use the table at the right. What is the mean tip for each of the days?

b. Suppose Server 2 keeps her own tips. Does she get more for the week? Explain.

Tips

Day	Server				
	1	2	3	4	5
Monday	$3.55	$6.20	$4.70	$3.85	$4.95
Tuesday	$5.10	$5.20	$5.70	$3.15	$3.55
Wednesday	$7.25	$8.30	$4.00	$6.20	$5.85
Thursday	$4.05	$2.10	$7.60	$2.75	$8.40
Friday	$9.75	$8.50	$9.25	$6.20	$7.35

2. On Saturday, Server 4 forgets to count her tips. Server 3 gathers all of the tip money and distributes an equal share to each server.

Tips

Server 1	Server 2	Server 3	Server 4	Server 5	Mean
$5.65	$6.80	$4.45	■	$7.55	$6.50

a. How much tip money did Server 4 receive originally? Explain.

b. Suppose the mean is $7.75. How much tip money did Server 4 receive originally?

Use the table on the next page for Exercises 3–6.

3. a. What is the mean amount of caffeine in the soda drinks?

b. Make a line plot for the soda drinks.

c. What is the mean amount of caffeine in the other drinks?

d. Make a line plot for the other drinks.

e. Write three statements comparing the amount of caffeine in soda and in other drinks.

4. Indicate whether each statement is true or false.

  a. Soda B has more caffeine than Soda F or Soda D.

  b. Energy Drink C has about three times as much caffeine as the same amount of Energy Drink A.

  c. Of the drinks in the table, 75% have 25 mg or less of caffeine in an 8-ounce serving.

Caffeine Content of Selected Beverages

Soda Drinks		Other Drinks	
Name	Caffeine in 8 Ounces (mg)	Name	Caffeine in 8 Ounces (mg)
Soda A	38	Energy Drink A	77
Soda B	37	Energy Drink B	70
Soda C	27	Energy Drink C	25
Soda D	27	Energy Drink D	21
Soda E	26	Iced Tea A	19
Soda F	24	Iced Tea B	10
Soda G	21	Coffee Drink	83
Soda H	15	Hot Cocoa	2
Soda J	23	Juice Drink	33

5. Moderate caffeine intake for adults is 300 mg per day, but it is recommended that 10- to 12-year-olds have no more than 85 mg per day. Has a middle-school student who drinks three 12-ounce cans of Soda F consumed more of his or her recommended intake of caffeine than an adult who drinks two servings of Coffee Drink?

6. Predict whether or not the mean and the median for caffeine content in the graph below have almost the same values. Explain.

Caffeine in Drinks

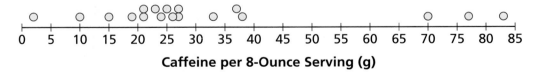

Caffeine per 8-Ounce Serving (g)

7. a. Compare the three sets of data. Which group of students has longer names? Explain your reasoning.

Name Length—30 Students From Japan

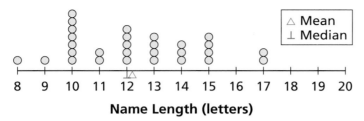

Name Length (letters)

Name Length—30 Students From Russia

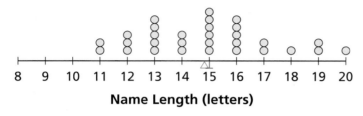

Name Length (letters)

Name Length—30 Students From the United States

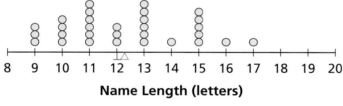

Name Length (letters)

b. Look at the distribution for the 30 students in the United States. Suppose the data for the six names with 13 letters were each changed to 16 letters.

   i. Draw a plot showing this change.

   ii. Will this change affect the median name length? Explain.

   iii. Will this change affect the mean name length? Explain.

Will this change affect the mean name length?

8. a. The next plots group the same 90 name lengths by gender. Compare the two plots. Which group of students has longer names? Explain.

Homework
Help ●nline
━━PHSchool.com
For: Help with Exercise 8
Web Code: ane-8208

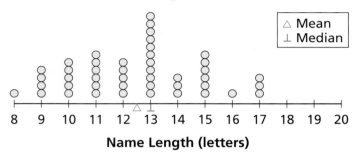

Name Lengths—Males

△ Mean
⊥ Median

Name Length (letters)

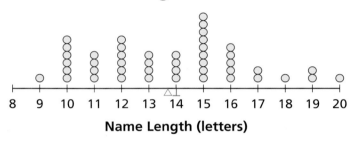

Name Lengths—Females

Name Length (letters)

b. Look at the distribution for the females. Suppose that the data for four names with 18 or more letters were changed. These students now each have name lengths with 10 or fewer letters.

  i. Draw a plot showing this change.

  ii. Will this change affect the median name length for females?

  iii. Will this change affect the mean name length for females?

9. Multiple Choice Send It Quick Mail House mailed five packages with a mean weight of 6.7 pounds. Suppose the mean weight of four of these packages is 7.2 pounds. What is the weight, in pounds, of the fifth package?

   A. 3.35   **B.** 4.7   **C.** 6.95   **D.** 8.7

10. **Multiple Choice** In test trials for two new sneaker designs, performance was judged by measuring jump heights. The results are shown below.

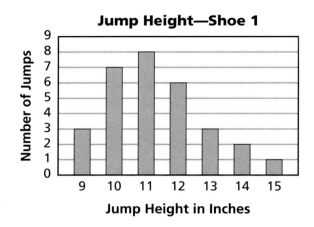

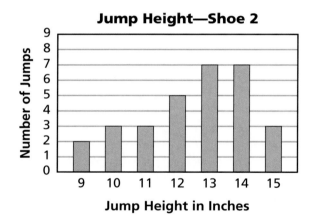

Which response below helps the shoe designer decide which sneaker, Shoe 1 or Shoe 2, performs better?

F. Use the mode. The most frequent height jumped for Shoe 1 was 11 inches. The most frequent height jumped for Shoe 2 was 13 or 14 inches.

G. Use the mean. The average jump height for Shoe 1 was 11.3 inches. For Shoe 2, the average was 12.5 inches.

H. Use clusters. Overall, 70% of the students jumped 10 to 12 inches with Shoe 1 while the data varied from 9 to 15 inches. About 63% of the students jumped 12 to 14 inches with Shoe 2 while the data varied from 9 to 15 inches.

J. All of the above.

11. a. What aspect of the shape of a distribution tells you that the mean is greater than the median? Explain.

   b. What aspect of the shape of a distribution tells you that the mean is less than the median? Explain.

   c. What aspect of the shape of a distribution tells you that the mean and the median are about the same value? Explain.

12. Multiple Choice Del Kenya's test scores are 100, 83, 88, 96, and 100. His teacher tells the class that they can choose the measure of center she will use to determine final grades. Which measure should Del Kenya choose?

For: Multiple-Choice Skills Practice
Web Code: ana-8254

   A. Mean   **B.** Median   **C.** Mode   **D.** Range

Connections

13. a. A gymnast receives these scores from five judges:

   7.6   8.2   8.5   8.2   8.9

   What happens to the mean of the scores when you multiply each data value by 2? By $\frac{2}{3}$? By 0.2?

   b. Why do you think the mean changes as it does in each situation?

ATHENS 2004

14. Multiple Choice Suppose a number is selected at random from a set of data. The data set has an even number of data values, no two of which are alike. What is the probability that this number will be greater than the median?

F. $\frac{1}{4}$ G. $\frac{5}{8}$ H. $\frac{1}{2}$ J. 1

15. Brilliant Candle Company claims their candles have longer mean burning times than those of other companies. Jaime chooses the same size candles from Brilliant Candle, Firelight Candle, and Shimmering Candle. He burns 15 candles from each company and records the number of minutes that each candle burns.

Burning Time (min)

Candle Number	Brilliant Candle	Firelight Candle	Shimmering Candle
1	60	66	68
2	49	68	65
3	58	56	44
4	57	59	59
5	61	61	51
6	53	64	60
7	57	53	61
8	60	51	63
9	61	60	49
10	62	50	56
11	60	64	59
12	56	60	62
13	61	60	64
14	59	51	57
15	58	49	54

For each company:

a. Make a line plot or bar graph for each company to display the distribution of the data.

b. Describe the variability within the set of data.

c. Estimate the mean and the median for each distribution.

d. Determine the mean and the median for each distribution. How do these values compare with your estimates in part (c)?

e. Do Brilliant Candle's products burn longer than the other two companies' products? Explain.

16. a. Make a circle graph that shows these results.

A survey about favorite colors reports that *exactly*:
 12% of those surveyed prefer red
 14% of those surveyed prefer orange
 28% of those surveyed prefer purple
 30% of those surveyed prefer blue
 16% of those surveyed prefer green

b. What is the smallest number of people that could have taken the survey? Explain.

Extensions

17. A student gets 40 points out of 100 points on a test. Her teacher announces that this test and next week's test will be averaged together for her grade. The student wonders if she could still get a C if she gets a 100 on the next test. She reasons, "I think my average (mean) would be 70 because half of 40 is 20 and half of 100 is 50. That is a C because 20 plus 50 is 70." Does her method always work? Explain your thinking.

18. If you know the number of chirps made by a cricket in a specific amount of time, you can estimate the temperature in degrees Fahrenheit or degrees Celsius. There are different ways you might do this. For example, one formula involves counting the chirps (the number of wing vibrations per second) over a 13-second period and adding 40 to get the temperature in degrees Fahrenheit. This formula works for the snowy tree cricket.

a. It is possible to turn cricket-chirp recordings into sound intensity versus time graphs. Then you can see each individual chirp and the chirp rate. Look at the four graphs below. Describe how you can tell that the chirp rates vary with the changes in temperature.

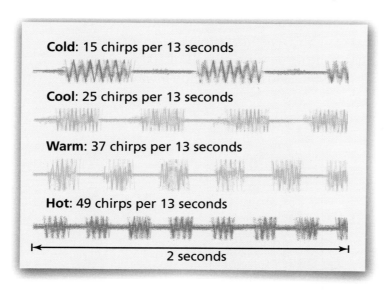

b. Another formula for estimating the temperature is more complicated. Count the chirps per minute, subtract 40, divide by 4, and add 50 to get the temperature in degrees Fahrenheit. Write this formula using x for the number of chirps per minute.

$$y = \text{Temperature in } °F = \underline{\quad ? \quad}$$

c. Use your formula from part (b). Draw a line on a coordinate graph that will allow you to relate the number of chirps per minute to temperatures from 0°F to 212°F. Use this line to predict the number of chirps expected for each temperature.

| 0°F | 50°F | 100°F | 212°F |

19. a. The chirp frequency for a different kind of cricket lets you estimate temperatures in Celsius rather than in Fahrenheit. Make a coordinate graph of the data below.

Cricket Chirps per Minute

Frequency	Temperature (°C)
195	31.4
123	22
212	34.1
176	29.1
162	27
140	24
119	20.9
161	27.8
118	20.8
175	28.5
161	26.4
171	28.1
164	27
174	28.6
144	24.6

b. Determine a formula that lets you estimate the temperature in degrees Celsius for a given number of chirps.

c. Use the formula from part (b) to draw a line on the graph from part (a). Describe how well the line "matches" the data. Explain your thinking.

Mathematical Reflections 2

In this investigation, you explored three measures of center. These questions will help you summarize what you have learned.

Think about your answers to these questions. Discuss your ideas with other students and your teacher. Then write a summary of your findings in your notebook.

1. **a.** Explain how the mean can be interpreted as an equal share in a situation. Use examples.

   b. Explain how the mean can be interpreted as a balance point in a distribution. Use examples.

   c. In what kinds of situations can you use the mode, but not the mean or the median, to identify what is typical? Use examples.

2. Give an example of each method of summarizing data. Explain why you might choose to use this method with your example.

   a. clusters   **b.** mode

   c. median   **d.** mean

3. **a.** When the mean and the median are the same or very similar, what does this indicate about the shape of the distribution?

   b. When the mean and median are more different than similar, what does this indicate about the shape of the distribution?

   c. Medians and means are called measures of center. Why do you think this is so?

Comparing Distributions: Equal Numbers of Data Values

Time is a measure that is used to answer many questions.

What was your time running a 50-yard dash or swimming 100 meters?

How fast is your reaction time to respond to events in a game?

Do wood roller coaster rides last longer than steel roller coaster rides?

You often compare times different people or groups take to complete a task. Think back to *Comparing and Scaling* and the ways you made comparisons between numbers using fractions, percents, and ratios. These ideas will help you make comparisons in data situations.

3.1 Measuring and Describing Reaction Times

When you hear, see, or touch something, a message is sent to the area of the brain that controls muscle activity. Then, a signal is sent out to muscles to respond. Sometimes it matters how quickly you react, for example:

- Swinging at a baseball with a bat or at a tennis ball with a racquet
- Swerving to miss a rock in the road while riding your bicycle
- Responding to actions in a video game

Computer programs can be used to test how quickly people react. For one such program, each trial begins with a colored circle appearing on the screen. When the circle appears, the person clicks on the circle as quickly as possible. When the trial is over, the person's time is reported.

Each student in a seventh-grade class completed five trials on a computer reaction-time game. In Problem 3.1, you will make comparisons among their reaction times.

Problem **3.1** **Measuring and Describing Reaction Times**

A. Write three different statements that describe the variability in Jasmine's times.

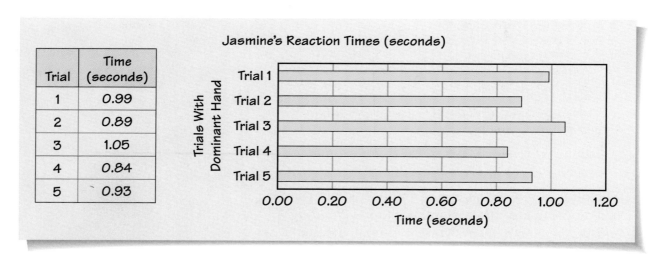

Jasmine's Reaction Times (seconds)

Trial	Time (seconds)
1	0.99
2	0.89
3	1.05
4	0.84
5	0.93

B. 1. Write three different statements that describe the variability in Nathaniel's times.

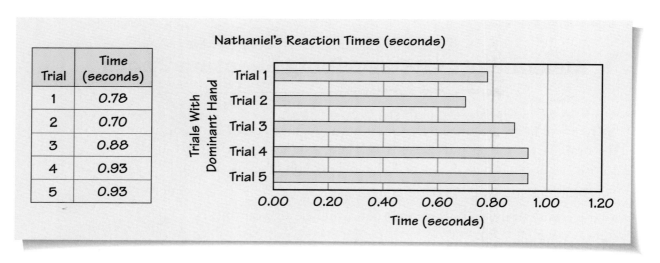

Nathaniel's Reaction Times (seconds)

Trial	Time (seconds)
1	0.78
2	0.70
3	0.88
4	0.93
5	0.93

2. How do Nathaniel's and Jasmine's results compare? Remember, you can use fractions, percents, and ratios to make comparisons.

ACE Homework starts on page 62.

The value bar graphs and data tables below show the computer game reaction times for Diana and Henry.

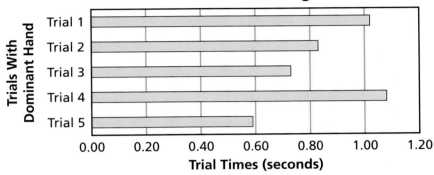

Diana—Female, Age 12

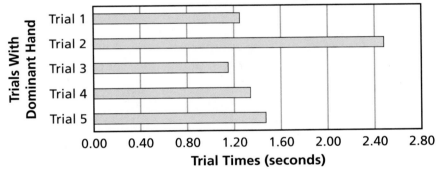

Henry—Male, Age 13

Diana's Reaction Times

Trial	1	2	3	4	5
Seconds	1.02	0.83	0.73	1.08	0.59

Henry's Reaction Times

Trial	1	2	3	4	5
Seconds	1.25	2.48	1.15	1.34	1.47

Who reacted faster, Diana or Henry?

When comparing performances, you can use variability, measures of center, and fraction, percent, or ratio statements.

A. In the four bar graphs on the next page, each student's data are shown on the same scale. What is the advantage of having the same scale on each graph?

B. 1. What are the minimum and maximum reaction times for each of the four students?

    2. What is the range of reaction times for each of the students?

    3. Does comparing ranges of reaction times help you decide if one student is more consistent than another student?

    4. Does comparing ranges of reaction times help you decide if one student is quicker than another student?

C. 1. What is the median reaction time for each student?

    2. What is the mean reaction time for each student?

    3. Does comparing mean or median reaction times help you decide whether one student is more consistent than another student?

    4. Does comparing mean or median reaction times help you decide whether one student is quicker than another student?

D. Locate 1 second on each graph. Explain how comparing data below, at, or above the benchmark time of 1 second can help determine whether one student is quicker than another student.

E. Another class has challenged this class to choose one student to play the computer reaction-time game against their class champion. Would you recommend they choose Diana, Henry, Nathaniel, or Jasmine? Why?

ACE Homework starts on page 62.

Jasmine's Reaction Times

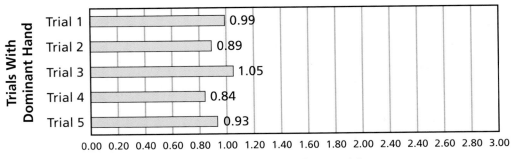

Trials With Dominant Hand	
Trial 1	0.99
Trial 2	0.89
Trial 3	1.05
Trial 4	0.84
Trial 5	0.93

Trial Times (seconds)

Nathaniel's Reaction Times

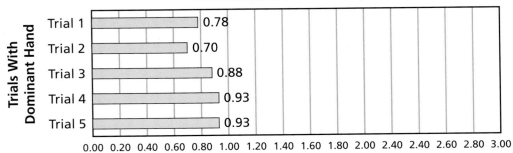

Trials With Dominant Hand	
Trial 1	0.78
Trial 2	0.70
Trial 3	0.88
Trial 4	0.93
Trial 5	0.93

Trial Times (seconds)

Diana—Female, Age 12

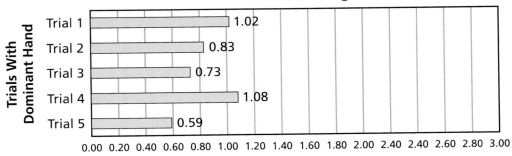

Trials With Dominant Hand	
Trial 1	1.02
Trial 2	0.83
Trial 3	0.73
Trial 4	1.08
Trial 5	0.59

Trial Times (seconds)

Henry—Male, Age 13

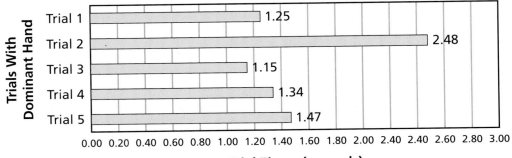

Trials With Dominant Hand	
Trial 1	1.25
Trial 2	2.48
Trial 3	1.15
Trial 4	1.34
Trial 5	1.47

Trial Times (seconds)

3.3 Comparing More Than a Few Students

For Problem 3.3, you will use a set of 40 case cards showing reaction times for a computer game. Copies of these cards can be found behind the Glossary.

Getting Ready for Problem

How can you locate each piece of information about a student on a case card?

Name	Trial 1 reaction time
Gender	Trial 2 reaction time
Age	Trial 3 reaction time
Fastest Time for 5 trials	Trial 4 reaction time
Slowest Time for 5 trials	Trial 5 reaction time

- Which attributes are categorical data?
- Which attributes are numerical data?
- Which attributes have values that vary from one student to another? Why do you think this is so?
- Which attributes have constant (the same) values for several or all of the students? Why do you think this is so?

Problem 3.3 Comparing Many Data Values

Use the reaction-time data to help you answer these questions.

A. Compare the distributions of the girls' fastest times and the boys' fastest times.

    1. Is one group more consistent? Explain.

    2. Is one group quicker? Explain.

B. Compare the distributions of the girls' slowest times and the boys' slowest times.

    1. Is one group more consistent? Explain.

    2. Is one group quicker? Explain.

ACE Homework starts on page 62.

Comparing Fastest and Slowest Trials

Willa is a video-game designer. You will help her make some decisions about timing in her video game.

Problem **3.4** **Comparing Larger Distributions**

Use the reaction time data to help you answer these questions.

A. Compare the fastest reaction times of all the students to the slowest reaction times of all the students. What must be true about the scales of the two line plots in order to make these comparisons easy to make?

B. 1. Describe how the means and the medians compare.

2. Describe how the ranges compare.

3. Where do the data cluster in each distribution? Describe how the locations of data clusters compare.

4. Is one distribution more variable than the other? Explain.

C. For each distribution, look at 0.5 second, 1 second, 1.5 seconds, and 2 seconds. Compare the numbers of students at, above, or below each of these benchmark times on each distribution. What do you notice?

D. Write a recommendation to Willa. Based on your work in Questions B and C, how much time should she give a player to react in a video game? Include recommendations for easy, medium, and hard levels. Justify your recommendations.

ACE Homework starts on page 62.

Applications

1. Write three different statements that describe the variability in Frank's reaction times.

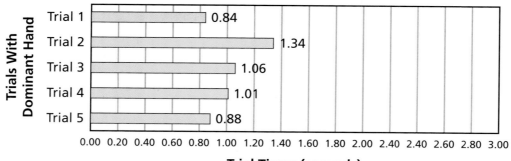

Frank's Reaction Times

Trials With Dominant Hand

Trial 1 — 0.84
Trial 2 — 1.34
Trial 3 — 1.06
Trial 4 — 1.01
Trial 5 — 0.88

0.00 0.20 0.40 0.60 0.80 1.00 1.20 1.40 1.60 1.80 2.00 2.40 2.40 2.60 2.80 3.00

Trial Times (seconds)

2. Compare Matthew's reaction times to Frank's reaction times.

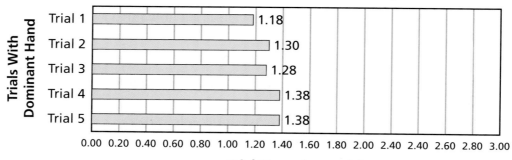

Matthew's Reaction Times

Trials With Dominant Hand

Trial 1 — 1.18
Trial 2 — 1.30
Trial 3 — 1.28
Trial 4 — 1.38
Trial 5 — 1.38

0.00 0.20 0.40 0.60 0.80 1.00 1.20 1.40 1.60 1.80 2.00 2.40 2.40 2.60 2.80 3.00

Trial Times (seconds)

a. Determine the means, medians, minimum and maximum values, and ranges for each student.

b. Is one student quicker than the other student? Explain your reasoning.

c. Is one student more consistent than the other student? Explain.

Graph A and Graph B show the fastest reaction time on a computer
reaction-time game with the non-dominant hand for each of the
40 students. Use these graphs for Exercises 3 and 4.

Graph A: Non-Dominant Hand Reaction Times

Fastest Time (seconds)

Graph B: Non-Dominant Hand Reaction Times

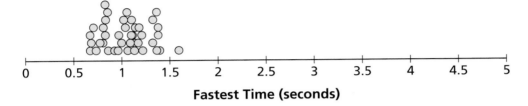

Fastest Time (seconds)

3. Tanisha says that Graph A and Graph B show the same data. Jeff says,
"No way! These are not the same data." Do you agree with Jeff?
Explain.

4. a. Use the statistics below and Graphs A and B above. Describe the
distribution of fastest reaction times using the non-dominant hand.

Mean:	1.06 seconds
Median:	1.08 seconds
Minimum Value:	0.68 second
Maximum Value:	1.60 seconds
Range:	0.92 seconds

b. How would you answer the question, "What is the typical fastest
reaction time for a student who uses his or her non-dominant hand?"

5. a. Describe the distribution of the data below.

Slowest Reaction Times With Non-Dominant Hand

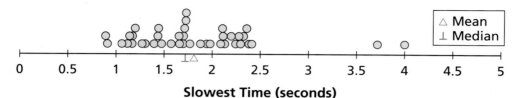

Slowest Time (seconds)

Mean:	1.82 seconds
Median:	1.73 seconds
Minimum Value:	0.90 second
Maximum Value:	4.01 seconds
Range:	3.11 seconds

b. How would you answer the question, "What is the typical slowest reaction time for a student who uses his or her non-dominant hand?" Explain.

6. Use the data in Exercise 5 and the data below to compare the fastest reaction times to the slowest reaction times for non-dominant hands. Explain your reasoning.

Fastest Reaction Times With Non-Dominant Hand

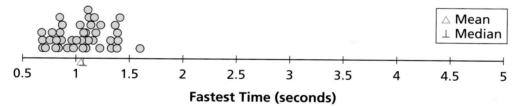

Fastest Time (seconds)

Mean:	1.06 seconds
Median:	1.08 seconds
Minimum Value:	0.68 second
Maximum Value:	1.60 seconds
Range:	0.92 second

7. Use the data from Exercises 5 and 6 and from the table on the facing page. Write statements to compare the values of each statistic for dominant and non-dominant hands.

a. means of the fastest reaction times

b. medians of the slowest reaction times

c. minimum and maximum values of the fastest reaction times

d. ranges of the fastest reaction times

Dominant Hand Reaction Times

Statistic	Fastest Reaction Times (seconds)	Slowest Reaction Times (seconds)
Mean	0.81	1.29
Median	0.79	1.22
Minimum Value	0.58	0.84
Maximum Value	1.18	2.48
Range	0.60	1.64

8. Use the line plots and table below. How much slower are the Trial 1 reaction times for non-dominant hands than the Trial 1 reaction times for dominant hands? Explain.

Homework Help Online
PHSchool.com
For: Help with Exercise 8
Web Code: ane-8308

Trial 1 Reaction Times With Dominant Hand

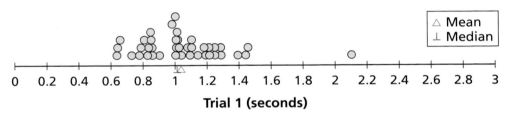

Trial 1 Reaction Times With Non-Dominant Hand

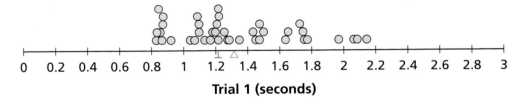

Trial 1 Reaction Times

Statistic	Dominant Hand (seconds)	Non-Dominant Hand (seconds)
Mean	1.048	1.324
Median	1.015	1.22
Minimum Value	0.64	0.83
Maximum Value	2.10	2.14
Range	1.50	1.31

Connections

9. Multiple Choice Suppose 27 is added as a data value to the set of data: 10, 29, 15, 29, 35, and 2. Which statement is true?

A. The mean increases by 4.　　　　**B.** The mode decreases by 10.

C. The median decreases by 1.　　　**D.** Not here

10. Multiple Choice The mean of six numbers is 25. If one number is 15, what is the mean of the other five numbers?

F. 15　　　　**G.** 25　　　　**H.** 27　　　　**J.** 40

For Exercises 11–13, look at the mean and median for the data. Describe how the shape of each distribution is influencing the location of the mean and the median. Explain your reasoning.

11. Mean = 62 inches, Median = 62 inches,
Minimum and Maximum Values = 53 and 72 inches

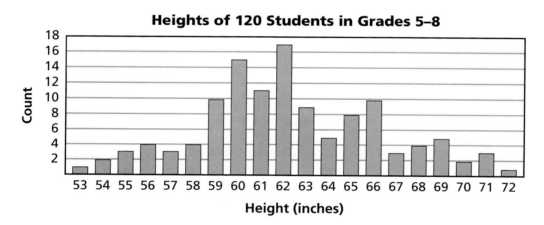

Heights of 120 Students in Grades 5–8

12. Mean = 24.7 grams, Median = 22.1 grams,
Minimum and Maximum Values = 21.3 and 37.1 grams

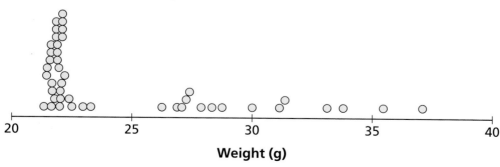

Weights of 45 Boxes of Cereal

13. Mean = 120.5 minutes, Median = 121 minutes,
Minimum and Maximum Values = 81 and 234 minutes

Runtimes for 100 of the Highest-Income Movies

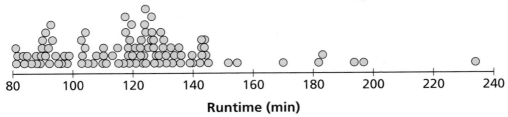

Runtime (min)

SOURCE: www.worldwideboxoffice.com

Use this graph for Exercises 14–16.

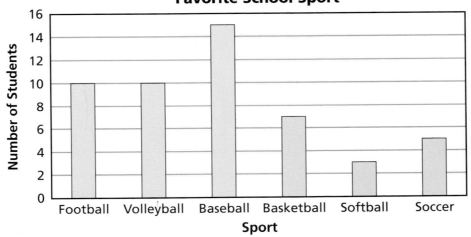

14. Multiple Choice Suppose a circle graph is used to display this data.
What percent of the circle graph would represent baseball and
softball?

A. 50%   **B.** 36%   **C.** 10%   **D.** 18%

15. Multiple Choice What fraction of a circle graph would include the
students who choose soccer?

F. $\frac{2}{5}$ **G.** $\frac{3}{25}$ **H.** $\frac{30}{100}$ **J.** $\frac{10}{100}$

16. Multiple Choice What would be the measure of the central angle
for the "volleyball" sector of a circle graph?

A. 20°   **B.** 36°   **C.** 72°   **D.** 18°

For: Multiple-Choice Skills
Practice
Web Code: ana-8354

17. Elisa receives these four graphs showing her family's water usage.

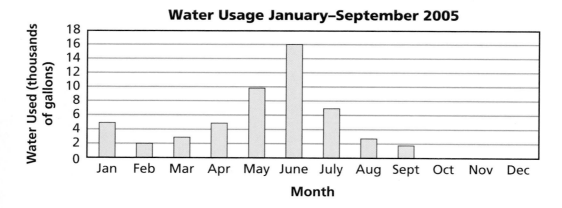

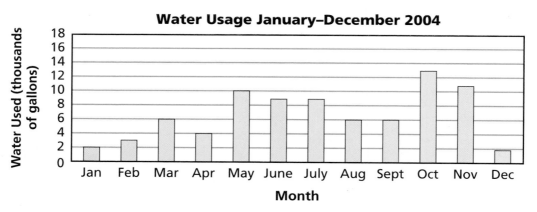

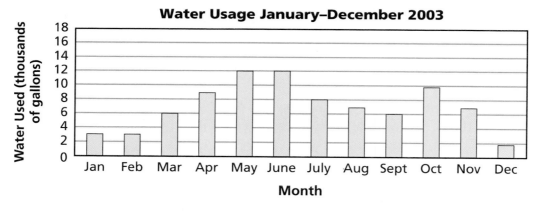

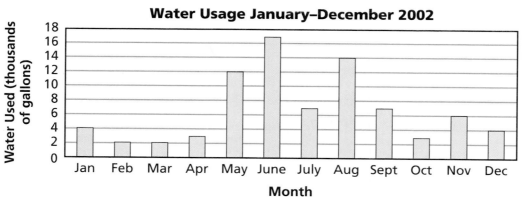

a. Describe any patterns in water usage that occur across years.

b. Use the graphs to find out how many gallons of water were used each month. Make a line plot for each of the years from 2003 to 2005 to show the distribution of the number of gallons used each month. For example, this line plot shows the data from 2002.

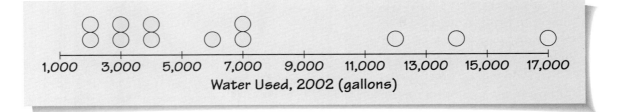

Water Used, 2002 (gallons)

c. Use the plots from part (b) to determine the mean monthly water usage for each year from 2002–2004. Mark these values on the plots. Using the mean monthly number of gallons used for each year, how does the water usage compare across the years? Explain.

d. Repeat part (c) for the median monthly water usage instead of the mean. Why should we not use the line plot for 2005 to estimate the mean or median?

e. Copy the data from your graphs in part (b) onto one line plot. You should have 45 data points. Determine the mean and the median for this new set of data. How do these two values compare? Why do you think this is so?

f. Is the median or the mean a better estimate of the typical monthly amount of water used during a year? Explain.

For Exercises 18–22, answer each question for each statement below.

Statement A
Garter snakes are the most typical snakes in North America. Fully grown, they can be 18 – 42 inches in length. They are generally about 3 feet long with a 1-inch girth. Although their coloring can be various shades of green, blue, brown, or red, they all have a pale but conspicuous stripe along the middle of the back and a less prominent stripe along each side.

Statement B
Each man, woman, and child in America eats an average of 46 slices (23 pounds) of pizza a year.

18. How do you think the process of data analysis was carried out?

19. What kinds of data—numerical or categorical—are used?

20. What kinds of variability might there be in the original data?

21. What kinds of patterns appear to have occurred in the data?

22. What is typical about the data and what might be outliers?

23. Multiple Choice A bag contains 36 chips. Each chip is either red or black. The probability of selecting a red chip from the bag is one fourth. What is the probability of drawing a black chip?

F. $\frac{1}{4}$ **G.** $\frac{3}{5}$ **H.** $\frac{7}{8}$ **J.** $\frac{3}{4}$

24. Write a title that provides the viewer with a summary snapshot of the information provided in the graph. Be clever. Do not just restate the data.

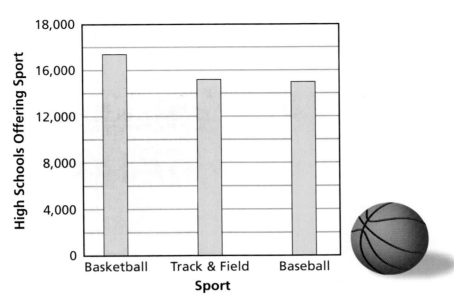

SOURCE: *National Federation of State High School Associations*

Extensions

25a. The line plot below shows the median reaction times for the students in Problem 3.3. Describe the distribution of the median reaction times.

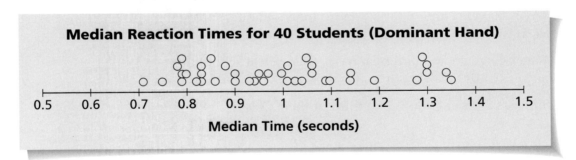

b. How do the median reaction times compare with the fastest reaction times, shown below?

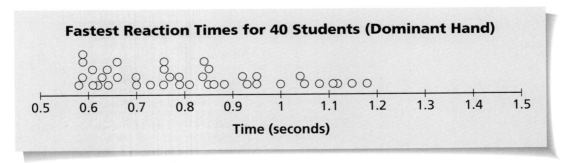

Use the circle graphs to determine whether each statement in Exercises 26–29 is true. For each statement that is not true, explain how you would change the statement to make it a true statement.

Daily Food Consumption

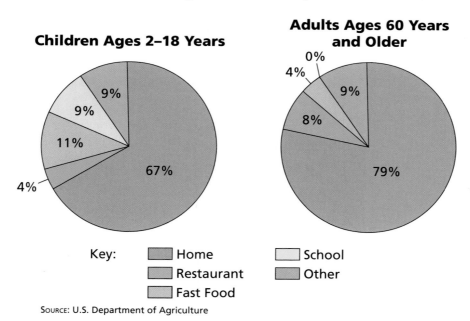

Children Ages 2–18 Years

Adults Ages 60 Years and Older

Key: Home   School
       Restaurant   Other
       Fast Food

Source: U.S. Department of Agriculture

26. Adults ages 60 years and older eat twice as many Calories at restaurants as do children ages 2–18.

27. Adults ages 60 years and older eat more than one quarter of their daily Calories at locations that are not their homes.

28. Adults ages 60 years and older eat more Calories at school than do children ages 2–18.

29. Children ages 2–18 eat about one third of their Calories at home.

Mathematical Reflections 3

In this investigation, you compared distributions of data with the same numbers of data values. These questions will help you summarize what you have learned.

Think about your answers to these questions. Discuss your ideas with other students and your teacher. Then write a summary of your findings in your notebook.

1. Sometimes you need to compare two or more distributions, each of which is shown on a different graph. Why is it helpful to make the scales of the axes the same on each graph?

2. Explain what a value bar graph and a line plot are. How are they related?

3. In several places you were asked to compare one or more students' reaction times. Use Henry's and Nathaniel's data from Problems 3.1 and 3.2. Describe how you can use fractions, percents, and ratios to make comparisons.

4. You also made comparisons among students' data to decide when one or more students were more consistent or quicker than other students.

   a. What does consistency mean when it refers to reaction times?

   b. What does quickness mean when it refers to reaction times?

   c. Identify a different situation in which you would compare consistency or quickness in performance. What does consistency or quickness mean in this situation?

Comparing Distributions: Unequal Numbers of Data Values

Many people love to ride roller coasters. There are different types of roller coasters, and people have preferences about the roller coasters they ride. In this investigation, you will look at data about roller coasters, and compare wood roller coasters with steel roller coasters.

4.1 Representing Survey Data

These two questions were asked in a survey.

1. Where do you like to sit on a roller coaster (choose one)?

___ Front ___ Middle ___ Back

2. Which of the following do you prefer to have on a roller coaster (may choose more than one)?

___ Airtime ___ Height ___ Inversions ___ Smooth Ride ___ Speed

The table below summarizes results from the survey and from three classes of seventh-grade students.

Roller Coaster Seating Preferences

Preference	Votes From Survey	Votes From Three Seventh-Grade Classes
Front	97	27
Middle	50	22
Back	18	14
Total Votes	**165**	**63**

Preferences for Roller Coaster Characteristics

Preference	Votes From Survey	Votes From Three Seventh-Grade Classes
Airtime	88	31
Height	36	24
Inversions	59	29
Smoothness	39	12
Speed	105	57
Total Votes	**327**	**153**

Problem 4.1 Representing Survey Data

A. Copy the tables above. Have the members of your class answer the two roller coaster questions. Add a column to each table for your class data.

B. Make bar graphs for each of the three data sets: the survey data, the data from the three classes, and the data from your class. Your bar graphs should allow you to compare the results from the three groups. You may use counts or percents to report frequencies.

C. Write three or more statements that make comparisons among the sets of data.

ACE Homework starts on page 78.

4.2 Are Steel Coasters Faster Than Wood Coasters?

Roller-coaster enthusiasts have preferences about the coasters they like to ride. There are Web sites devoted to wood roller coasters. Other people prefer to ride steel coasters.

Have you ever wondered how many roller coasters there are in the world? The table below shows roller coaster counts.

Roller Coaster Census (2005)

Continent	Total	Wood	Steel	Some of the Types of Steel Coasters			
				Inverted	Stand Up	Suspended	Sit Down
Africa	23	0	23	3	0	0	20
Asia	489	8	481	17	5	8	441
Australia	23	3	20	2	0	0	18
Europe	581	34	547	24	1	7	506
North America	748	131	617	50	11	10	531
South America	65	1	64	2	0	0	62
Total	1,929	177	1,752	98	17	25	1,578

Source: Roller Coaster DataBase. Go to www.PHSchool.com for a data update. Web Code: ang-9041

How do you think these data were collected?

In Problem 4.2, you will use a roller coaster database that contains data on 50 wood coasters and 100 steel coasters.

Problem 4.2 Comparing Speed

Use the Roller Coaster Database to help you answer these questions.

A. Choose an attribute about roller coasters that interests you, such as Year Opened, Maximum Drop, or Top Speed. Explore this attribute in the database. Write a short paragraph about what you find.

B. 1. What do you consider to be a fast speed for a roller coaster? Discuss your idea with a partner.

    2. Suppose you have to choose which of two roller coasters to ride. Does knowing the top speed for each coaster help you make the decision? Explain.

C. 1. Are wood roller coasters faster than steel roller coasters? Scan the *top speed* data to predict an answer to the question. Explain your reasoning.

   2. Now, look at the distributions of speeds of wood roller coasters and of steel roller coasters. Use strategies that make sense to you.

   a. Identify and compare minimum and maximum values, ranges, medians, and means for each type of roller coaster.

   b. Draw a reference line on each distribution at a particular speed. Look at the percents of each type of roller coaster at and above or below this speed.

   3. Compare your prediction from part (1) with your analysis of the distributions from part (2). How would you now answer the question, "Are wood roller coasters faster than steel roller coasters?" Explain.

D. Why do some roller coasters go faster than other roller coasters? To help answer this question, look at the top speed in relation to other attributes. Do you think there is some relationship between *top speed and maximum drop*? Between *top speed and maximum height*? Between *top speed and year opened, duration, track length, or angle of descent*? Explore these questions. Be prepared to share your reasoning.

active math
online
For: Stat Tools
Visit: PHSchool.com
Web Code: and–8402

ACE **Homework starts on page 78.**

Applications

1. This question was asked in a survey:

   What is your favorite kind of amusement-park ride?

   ___ Roller Coaster ___ Log Ride ___ Ferris Wheel ___ Other

   The table below summarizes results from this survey and from a survey of seventh-grade students at East Junior High and West Junior High.

Homework Help Online
PHSchool.com

For: Help with Exercise 1
Web Code: ane-8401

Favorite Amusement Park Rides

Favorite Ride	Votes From Survey	Votes From East Junior High	Votes From West Junior High
Roller Coaster	84	45	36
Log Ride	36	31	14
Ferris Wheel	17	3	6
Other	18	1	4
Total Votes	**155**	**80**	**60**

a. Make bar graphs for each of the three data sets: the survey data, the data from East Junior High, and the data from West Junior High. Your bar graphs should allow you to compare the results from the three groups. Use percents to report frequencies.

b. Write three or more statements that make comparisons among the sets of data.

2. The three pairs of line plots below display data about 50 wood roller coasters. Means and medians are marked on each graph.

Graph A: Maximum Drop for Each Wood Coaster

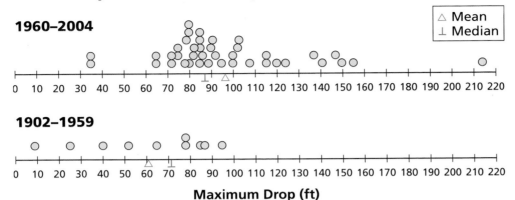

Graph B: Maximum Height for Each Wood Coaster

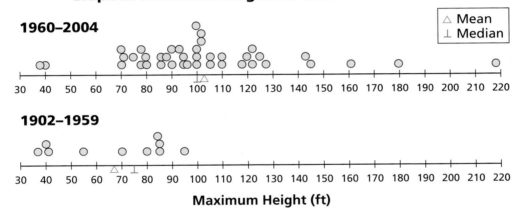

Graph C: Top Speed for Each Wood Coaster

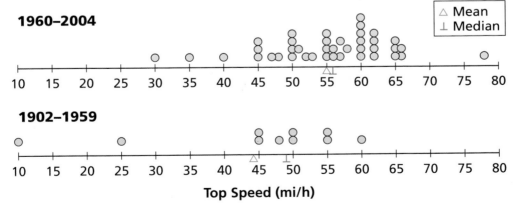

a. Write three statements comparing wood roller coasters built before 1960 with wood roller coasters built in 1960 or later.

b. Hector says there are too few roller coasters to make comparisons. Do you agree with Hector? Explain.

Use the Roller Coaster Census from Problem 4.2 for Exercises 3–7.

3. For every one wood roller coaster there are about ■ steel roller coasters.

4. North America has about ■ times as many roller coasters as South America.

5. Asia has about ■ as many roller coasters as North America.

6. North America has ■% of all the wood roller coasters in the world.

7. Write two of your own comparison statements.

Connections

8. The titles of the two circle graphs below have been separated from the graphs. Use the data from Exercises 3–7 to determine which title goes with which graph. Explain your reasoning.

Title 1: Wood Roller Coasters by Continent
Title 2: Steel Roller Coasters by Continent

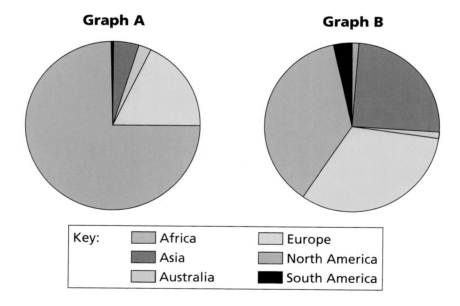

Graph A **Graph B**

Key: Africa Europe
      Asia North America
      Australia South America

9. Multiple Choice Jasper's test scores for eight exams are shown.

    84   72   88   84   92   94   78 x

If the median for his scores is 86, what is a possible value for x?

A. 68   **B.** 84   **C.** 86   **D.** 95

10. Multiple Choice In Mr. Ramirez's math class, there are three times as many girls as boys. The girls' mean grade on a quiz is 90 and the boys' mean grade is 86. What is the mean grade for the class altogether?

F. 88   **G.** 44   **H.** 89   **J.** 95

11. People in the movie business track box-office profits and compare gains and losses each week. The graph below compares box-office income for consecutive weekends in the fall of 2005. Did box-office profits increase or decrease? Explain your reasoning.

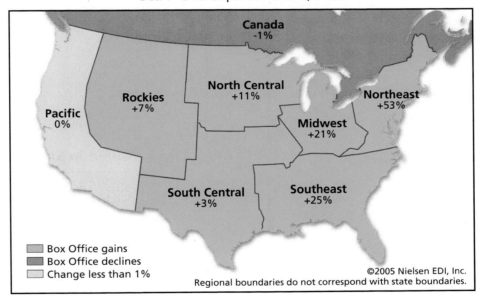

Regional Percentage Changes
Oct. 7–9 vs. Sept. 30–Oct. 2, 2005

12. In a large survey of nearly 15,000 children ages 5 to 15, 80% of the children were from the United States. Use the data below for parts (a)–(f).

Table 1: Years Lived in Current Home

Years	Children	Percent
<1	639	7.9%
1	776	9.6%
2	733	9.0%
3	735	▪
4	587	7.3%
5	612	7.5%
6	487	6.0%
7	431	5.3%
8	442	5.5%
9	412	5.1%
10	492	6.0%
11	520	6.5%
12	508	6.3%
13	339	4.1%
14	225	2.8%
15	176	2.2%
Total	**8,114**	**100.0%**

SOURCE: National Geographic

Table 2: Apartments or Houses Lived in Since Birth

Number of Apartments or Houses	Children	Percent
1	1,645	20.7%
2	1,957	24.7%
3	1,331	16.8%
4	968	▪
5	661	8.3%
6	487	6.1%
7	291	3.7%
8	184	2.3%
9	80	1.0%
10	330	4.2%
Total	**7,934**	**100.0%**

SOURCE: National Geographic

Table 3: Cities or Towns Lived in Since Birth

Number of Cities or Towns	Boys	Girls	Ages 5–12	Ages 13–15
1	▪	42.2%	42.1%	40.9%
>1	58.9%	57.8%	▪	59.1%
Total	**100%**	**100%**	**100%**	**100%**

SOURCE: National Geographic

a. Find the missing percents in the tables above. Explain how you determined your answers.

b. Make a bar graph displaying the information in the third column of Table 2.

c. Write a summary paragraph about Table 2.

d. What percent of children have lived in the same home for 10 or more years? Justify your answer.

e. What percent of the children have lived in only one home since they were born? Justify your answer.

f. About what fraction of the boys have lived in the same city or town all their lives? Explain.

The graph below shows the amount of sugar per serving in the 47 cereals. Use the graph for Exercises 13 and 14.

Amount of Sugar per Serving

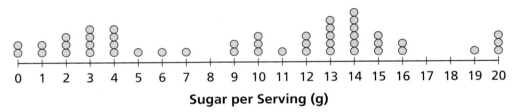

Sugar per Serving (g)

13. Describe the variability in the distribution of the amount of sugar per serving.

14. Estimate the locations of the mean and the median. How does the shape of the distribution influence your estimates?

The next graph shows the serving sizes of the 47 cereals in the graph above.

Serving Sizes of Cereals

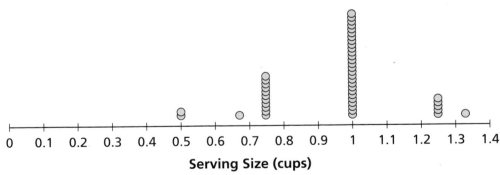

Serving Size (cups)

15. Describe the distribution of serving sizes.

16. Estimate the locations of the mean and the median. How does the shape of the distribution influence your estimates?

Extensions

17. a. Copy the scatter plot below. Locate the point $(443, 6)$ and circle it.

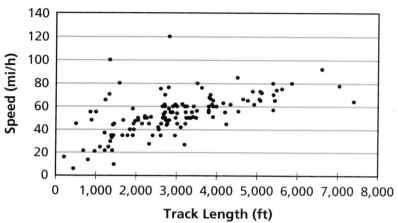

Track Length and Speed of 150 Wood and Steel Coasters

b. Locate the point $(6595, 92)$ and circle it.

c. Draw a line that connects these two points.

d. What is true about the points representing coasters that are on this line? That are above this line? That are below this line?

e. Using these two points, write an equation for the line in the form $y = mx$.

Mathematical Reflections 4

In this investigation, you developed strategies to compare two or more distributions with unequal amounts of data. These questions will help you summarize what you have learned.

Think about your answers to these questions. Discuss your ideas with other students and your teacher. Then write a summary of your findings in your notebook.

1. You can use different strategies to compare two or more data sets. Some strategies are listed below. Describe how each strategy helps you compare data sets. Add other strategies you would use to the list.

   a. Use the range for each distribution.

   b. Use the mean and median for each distribution.

   c. Use benchmarks to help you compare sections of distributions.

2. In Investigations 3 and 4, you compared groups by using counts to report actual frequencies or by using percents to report relative frequencies. How is your choice to use counts or percents affected by whether you are comparing distributions with equal numbers of data values or distributions with unequal numbers of data values? Explain.

Looking Back and Looking Ahead

Unit Review

Go Online
PHSchool.com

For: Vocabulary Review
Puzzle
Web Code: anj-8051

While working on the problems in this unit, you explored distributions of data, measures of center, and comparing groups. You explored ways to describe and make sense of the variability that is in all data.

You often need to compare two or more groups of data. Sometimes you can compare actual counts. Other times you need to use percents. In this unit, you looked at ways to compare both kinds of distributions.

Use Your Understanding: Statistical Reasoning

How do frozen pizzas compare with the real thing? The table on the next page displays some information about frozen pizza ratings.

1. Make a graph showing the number of Calories in one slice of each frozen pizza.

    a. What is the typical number of Calories per slice of pizza?

    b. Describe the variability in the number of Calories per slice of frozen pizza.

    c. Now, show separate distributions for cheese pizzas and for pepperoni pizzas. Compare the Calories in a slice of cheese pizza to those in a slice of pepperoni pizza. Do cheese pizzas have more Calories than pepperoni pizzas? Explain.

2. Make a graph showing the cost per slice of each frozen pizza.

    a. What is the typical cost per slice of pizza?

    b. Describe the variability in the cost per slice of frozen pizza.

    c. Now, show separate distributions for cheese pizzas and for pepperoni pizzas. Compare the cost of a slice of cheese pizza to that of a slice of pepperoni pizza. Do pepperoni pizzas cost more than cheese pizzas? Explain.

3. **a.** Make two scatter plots, one for (*fat grams, Calories*) data and one for (*cost, Calories*) data.

    b. What do you notice about the relationship between fat grams and Calories?

c. What do you notice about the relationship between cost and Calories?

d. Compare the relationships in parts (b) and (c). Which one seems "stronger"? Can you make predictions about the value of one variable if you know the value for another? Explain.

Frozen Pizza Ratings

Product	Overall Rating	Cost per Slice	Calories per Slice	Fat (g)
Cheese Pizza A	VG	$0.98	364	15
Cheese Pizza B	VG	$1.23	334	11
Cheese Pizza C	VG	$0.94	332	12
Cheese Pizza D	VG	$1.92	341	14
Cheese Pizza E	VG	$0.84	307	9
Cheese Pizza F	VG	$0.96	335	12
Cheese Pizza G	VG	$0.80	292	9
Cheese Pizza H	VG	$0.96	364	18
Cheese Pizza J	VG	$0.91	384	20
Cheese Pizza K	VG	$0.89	333	12
Cheese Pizza L	G	$0.94	328	14
Cheese Pizza M	G	$1.02	367	13
Cheese Pizza N	G	$0.92	325	13
Cheese Pizza P	G	$1.17	346	17
Cheese Pizza Q	F	$0.54	299	9
Cheese Pizza R	F	$1.28	394	19
Cheese Pizza S	F	$0.67	322	14
Pepperoni Pizza A	VG	$0.96	385	18
Pepperoni Pizza B	VG	$0.88	369	16
Pepperoni Pizza C	VG	$0.90	400	22
Pepperoni Pizza D	VG	$0.88	378	20
Pepperoni Pizza E	G	$0.89	400	23
Pepperoni Pizza F	G	$0.87	410	26
Pepperoni Pizza G	G	$1.28	412	25
Pepperoni Pizza H	F	$1.26	343	14
Pepperoni Pizza J	F	$1.51	283	6
Pepperoni Pizza K	F	$0.74	372	20
Pepperoni Pizza L	F	$0.64	367	20
Pepperoni Pizza M	F	$1.62	280	4

SOURCE: Consumer Reports

Explain Your Reasoning

When you describe a collection of data, you look for the shape of the distribution of the data. You can often visualize data patterns using graphs.

4. Explain how you would describe the variability in a distribution of data.

5. Describe how the location of the mean and the median are related to the shape of the distribution.

6. Describe strategies you can use to compare two groups of data that have equal numbers of data values.

7. Describe strategies you can use to compare two groups of data that have unequal numbers of data values.

8. What does it mean to say that the speed of a roller coaster *is related to* the maximum drop, or that the roller coaster rating *is related to* the speed of a roller coaster?

Look Ahead

You will use and extend ideas about data analysis in a variety of future *Connected Mathematics* units. In *Samples and Populations,* you will explore sampling, comparing samples, and comparing different variables in a sample. You will also find statistical plots and data summaries in everyday news reports as well as in the technical work of science, business, and government.

A

attribute A property, quality, or characteristic of a person, place, or thing. For example, each person has attributes such as height, weight, name, gender, and eye color.

atributo Propiedad, cualidad o característica de una persona, lugar o cosa. Por ejemplo, cada persona tiene atributos, como altura, peso, nombre, género y color de ojos.

C

categorical data Data that can be placed into categories. For example, "gender" is a categorical data and the categories are "male" and "female." If you asked people in which month they were born or what their favorite class is, they would answer with names, which would be categorical data. However, if you asked them how many siblings they have, they would answer with numbers, not categories.

datos categóricos Datos que pueden ser colocados en categorías. Por ejemplo, "género" es un dato categórico y las categorías son "masculino" y "femenino." Si le preguntas a la gente en qué mes nacieron o cual es su clase favorita, responderían con nombres, lo cual es un dato categórico. Sin embargo, si le preguntas cuántos hermanos o hermanas tienen, responderán con números, no con categorías.

counts Data that give the number of occurrences (the frequency) of an attribute, for example, the number of occurrences of 3-child families.

cuentas Datos que dan el número de veces que ocurre (frecuencia) un evento, por ejemplo, el número de familias que tienen 3 niños.

D

distribution Data sets collected from observation or experiment. They can be described by measures of center and variability.

distribución Conjuntos de datos reunidos a partir de la observación o la experimentación. Pueden ser descritos con medidas de tendencia central y variabilidad.

G

graphs Any pictorial device, such as a scatter plot or bar graph, used to display categorical or numerical data.

gráficas Cualquier elemento pictórico, como una gráfica de dispersión o una gráfica de barras, usado para mostrar datos categóricos numéricos.

line plot Each data value is represented as a dot or an "x" positioned over a labeled number line. The line plot made with dots is sometimes referred to as a dot plot.

diagrama de puntos Cada valor de datos es representado como un punto o una "x" ubicada sobre una recta numérica rotulada. El diagrama de puntos hecho con puntos algunas veces se conoce como gráfica de puntos.

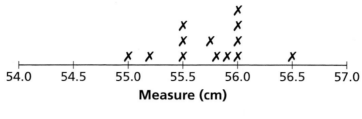

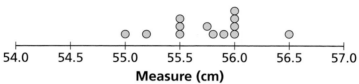

mean (1) The result if all of the data values are combined and then redistributed evenly among individuals so that each has the same amount. (2) The number that is the balance point in a distribution of numerical values. The mean is influenced by all of the values of the distribution, including outliers. It is often called the average, and is the sum of the numerical values divided by the number of values. For example, the mean of 1, 3, 7, 8, and 25 is 8.8 because the sum of the values, 44, is divided by the number of values, 5.

media (1) El resultado, si todos los valores de datos están combinados y luego redistribuidos uniformemente entre diferentes individuos, de modo que cada uno tenga la misma cantidad. (2) El número que es el punto de equilibrio en una distribución de valores numéricos. La media se ve afectada por todos los valores de la distribución, incluyendo los valores extremos. Por lo general se le llama promedio, es la suma de los valores numéricos dividida por el número de valores. Por ejemplo, la media de 1, 3, 7, 8 y 25 es 8.8 porque la suma de los valores, 44, se divide por el número de valores, 5.

measures Data obtained by making measurements. For example, we can measure the height of each person in a class.

medidas Datos obtenidos al hacer mediciones. Por ejemplo, podemos medir la altura de cada persona en una clase.

measures of center See *mean, median,* and *mode.*

medidas de tendencia central Ver *mean, median* y *mode.*

median The median is the number that is the midpoint of an ordered set of numerical data. This means that at least half of the data values lie at or above the median and at least half lie at or below it. For example, the median of 1, 3, 7, 8, and 25 is 7 because that number is third in the list of five data values. The median of 2, 3, 4, 4, 4, 5, 6, 12, and 13 is 4 because that number is fifth in the list of nine data values.

When a distribution contains an even number of data values, the median is computed by finding the average of the two middle data values in an ordered list of the data values. For example, the median of 1, 3, 7, 8, 25, and 30 is 7.5 because the data values 7 and 8 are third and fourth in the list of six data values.

mediana La mediana es el número que es el punto medio de un conjunto ordenado de datos numéricos. Esto significa que al menos la mitad de los valores de datos están en o sobre la mediana y al menos la mitad están en o bajo la mediana. Por ejemplo, la mediana de 1, 3, 7, 8 y 25 es 7, porque éste es tercer número en la lista de cinco valores de datos. La mediana de 2, 3, 4, 4, 4, 5, 6, 12 y 13 es 4, porque éste número es el quinto en la lista de nueve valores de datos.
Cuando una distribución contiene, un número par de valores de datos, la mediana se obtiene averiguando el promedio de los dos valores medios en una lista ordenada de valores de datos. Por ejemplo, la mediana de 1, 3, 7, 8, 25 y 30 es 7.5, porque los valores de datos 7 y 8 son tercero y cuarto en la lista de seis valores de datos.

mode The data value or category occurring with the greatest frequency. For example, the mode of 3, 4, 7, 11, 11, 11, 3, and 4 is 11.

moda El valor de dato o categoría que sucede con la mayor frecuencia. Por ejemplo, la moda de 3, 4, 7, 11, 11, 11, 3 y 4 es 11.

N

numerical data Data consisting of numbers, not categories, such as the heights of students.

dato numérico Dato que consiste en números, no categorías, tales como la altura de los estudiantes.

O

ordered value bar graph A value bar graph in which data values are arranged in increasing (or decreasing) order of length.

gráfica de barras con valores ordenados Gráfica de barras de valores en la cual los valores de los datos están ordenado en orden creciente (o decreciente).

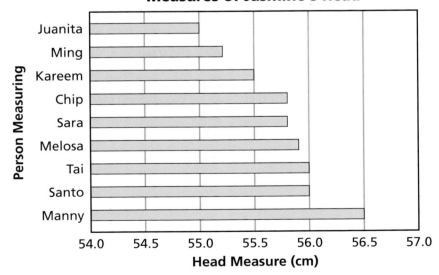

Measures of Jasmine's Head

outliers Unusually high or low data values in a distribution.

valores extremos o atípicos Valores de datos excepcionalmente altos o bajos en una distribución.

range A number found by subtracting the minimum value from the maximum value. If you know the range of the data is 12 grams of sugar per serving, you know that the difference between the minimum and maximum values is 12 grams.

rango Número que se halla al restar el valor mínimo del valor máximo. Si se sabe que el rango de los datos es 12 gramos de azúcar por porción, entonces se sabe que la diferencia entre el valor mínimo y el máximo es 12 gramos.

scatter plot A coordinate graph showing the relationship, if any, between two variables, for example, roller coaster track length and speed.

diagrama de dispersión Gráfica de coordenadas que muestra la relación, si la hay, entre dos variables, por ejemplo, largo de las vías de una montaña rusa y la velocidad.

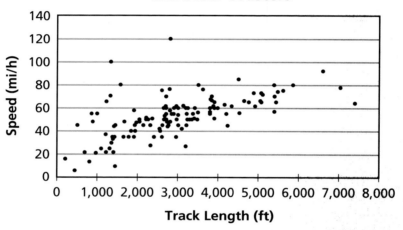

Track Length and Speed of 150 Wood and Steel Coasters

value of an attribute Values are the data that occur for each individual case of an attribute—that is, the number of red jellybeans recorded for the attribute red from one bag of jellybeans or the time in seconds recorded for the attribute fastest time for one student who played the computer reaction-time game.

valor de un atributo Los valores son los datos que suceden para cada *caso* independiente de un atributo, o sea, el número de caramelos rojos registrados para el atributo *rojo* de una bolsa de caramelos o el tiempo en segundos registrado para el atributo *tiempo más rápido* de un estudiante que jugó un juego de computadora de tiempo de reacción.

value bar graph Each data value is represented by a separate bar whose relative length corresponds to the magnitude of that data value.

gráfica de barras de valores Cada valor de dato se representa por una barra independiente, cuya longitud relativa corresponde con la magnitud de ese valor de dato.

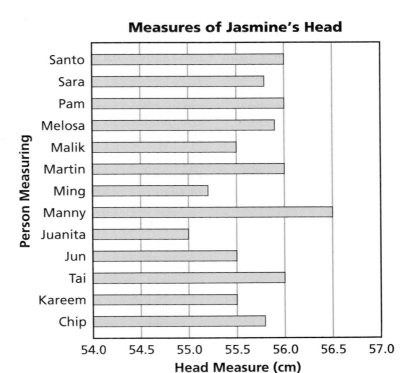

variability of a set of numerical data An indication of how widely spread or closely clustered the data values are. Range, minimum and maximum values, and clusters in the distribution give some indication of variability.

variabilidad de un conjunto de datos numéricos Indicación de cuán dispersos o conglomerados están los valores de datos. El rango, los valores mínimo y máximo, y las conglomeraciones en la distribución dan cierta indicación de variabilidad.

Academic Vocabulary

The following terms are important to your understanding of the mathematics in this unit. Knowing and using these words will help you in thinking, reasoning, representing, communicating your ideas, and making connections across ideas. When these words make sense to you, the investigations and problems will make more sense as well.

C

compare To tell or show how two things are alike and different.

related terms: analyze, relate

Sample: How do the mean and the median of this data compare?

Item	Number Sold
Pencil	100
Pen	20
Mouse Pad	10
Dictionary	5
Notebook	52

The mean of this data is $\frac{100 + 20 + 10 + 5 + 52}{5} = 37.4$. The median is 20. The mean is much greater than the median because the number of pencils sold is an outlier for this data.

comparar Decir o mostrar en qué se parecen o en qué se diferencian dos cosas.

términos relacionados: analizar, relacionar

Ejemplo: ¿Cómo se comparan la media y la mediana de estos datos?

Útil	Número vendido
Lápiz	100
Bolígrafo	20
Almohadilla para ratón	10
Diccionario	5
Cuaderno	52

La media de estos datos es $\frac{100 + 20 + 10 + 5 + 52}{5} = 37.4$. La mediana es 20. La media es mucho mayor que la mediana porque el número de lápices vendidos es un valor extremo de estos datos.

D

determine To use the given information and any related facts to find a value or make a decision.

related terms: decide, find, calculate, conclude

Sample: What can you determine about the variability of the data?

Pumpkin	1	2	3	4	5
Weight (lbs)	17	25	32	16	19

The range of the data is $32 - 16 = 16$ pounds. However, three of the weights are clustered in the teens: 16, 17, and 19 pounds.

determinar Usar la información dada y cualesquiera datos relacionados para hallar un valor o tomar una decisión.

términos relacionados: decidir, hallar, calcular, concluir

Ejemplo: ¿Qué puedes determinar sobre la variabilidad de los datos?

Calabaza	1	2	3	4	5
Peso (libras)	17	25	32	16	19

El rango de los datos es $32 - 16 = 16$ libras. Sin embargo, tres de los pesos están muy cerca uno de otro: 16, 17 y 19 libras.

explain To give facts and details that make an idea easier to understand. Explaining can involve a written summary supported by a diagram, chart, table, or a combination of these.

related terms: describe, show, justify, tell, present

Sample: Explain how to determine the median of the data set: 2, 7, 8, 1, 0, 7, 4, 1.

> To find the median, order all of the data points from least to greatest.
>
> 0, 1, 1, 2, 4, 7, 7, 8
>
> The value in the middle is the median. Since there are an even number of data, find the mean of the two middle values. For this data, the median is 3; because $(2 + 4) \div 2 = 3$.

explicar Dar datos y detalles que facilitan el entendimiento de una idea. Explicar puede requerir la preparación de un informe escrito apoyado por un diagrama, una tabla, un esquema o una combinación de éstos.

términos relacionados: describir, mostrar, justificar, decir, presentar

Ejemplo: Explica cómo se determina la mediana del conjunto de datos: 2, 7, 8, 1, 0, 7, 4, 1.

> Para hallar la mediana, ordena todos los puntos de datos de menor a mayor.
>
> 0, 1, 1, 2, 4, 7, 7, 8
>
> El valor del medio es la mediana. Como el número datos es par, halla la media de los dos valores del medio. Para estos datos, la mediana es 3, porque $(2 + 4) \div 2 = 3$.

---

relate To have a connection or impact on something else.

related terms: connect, correlate

Sample: Relate the data in the table to the value bar graph.

Plant	Height (cm)
1	52
2	50
3	42
4	67
5	48

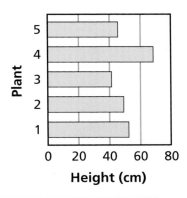

> The heights (cm) in the table are represented by the lengths of the bars in the bar graph. Each bar represents one of the plants. The plants' heights can be determined by looking at the values on the horizontal axis.

relacionar Haber una conexión o impacto entre una cosa y otra.

términos relacionados: unir, correlacionar

Ejemplo: Relaciona los datos de la tabla con la gráfica de barras de los valores.

Planta	Altura (cm)
1	52
2	50
3	42
4	67
5	48

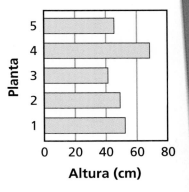

> Las alturas (cm) de la tabla están representadas por las longitudes de las barras que aparecen en la gráfica de barras. Cada barra representa una de las plantas. Las alturas de las plantas se pueden determinar observando los valores de la línea horizontal.

Reaction Time Cards

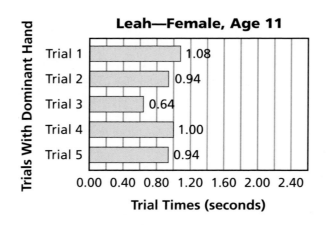

Leah—Female, Age 11

Trial	Trial Times (seconds)
Trial 1	1.08
Trial 2	0.94
Trial 3	0.64
Trial 4	1.00
Trial 5	0.94

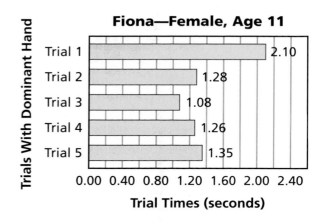

Fiona—Female, Age 11

Trial	Trial Times (seconds)
Trial 1	2.10
Trial 2	1.28
Trial 3	1.08
Trial 4	1.26
Trial 5	1.35

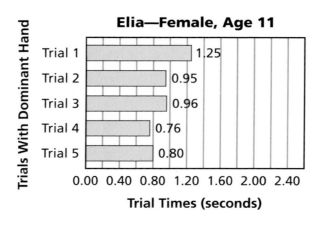

Elia—Female, Age 11

Trial	Trial Times (seconds)
Trial 1	1.25
Trial 2	0.95
Trial 3	0.96
Trial 4	0.76
Trial 5	0.80

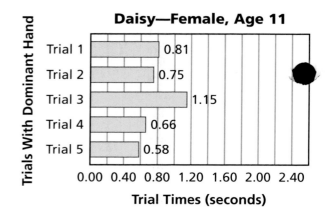

Daisy—Female, Age 11

Trial	Trial Times (seconds)
Trial 1	0.81
Trial 2	0.75
Trial 3	1.15
Trial 4	0.66
Trial 5	0.58

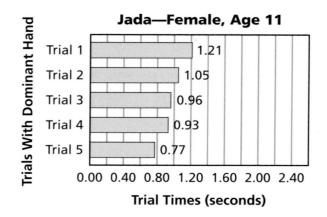

Jada—Female, Age 11

Trial	Trial Times (seconds)
Trial 1	1.21
Trial 2	1.05
Trial 3	0.96
Trial 4	0.93
Trial 5	0.77

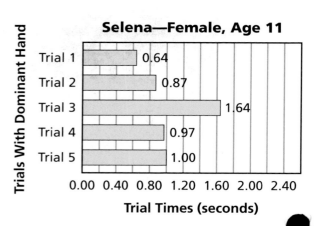

Selena—Female, Age 11

Trial	Trial Times (seconds)
Trial 1	0.64
Trial 2	0.87
Trial 3	1.64
Trial 4	0.97
Trial 5	1.00

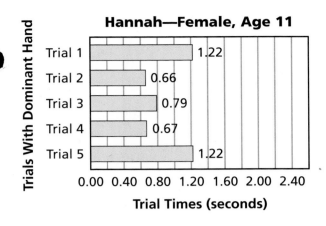

Hannah—Female, Age 11

Trials With Dominant Hand

Trial	Trial Times (seconds)
Trial 1	1.22
Trial 2	0.66
Trial 3	0.79
Trial 4	0.67
Trial 5	1.22

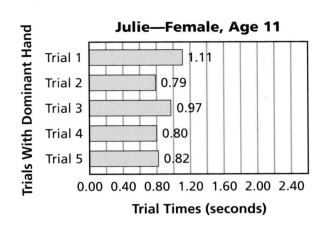

Julie—Female, Age 11

Trials With Dominant Hand

Trial	Trial Times (seconds)
Trial 1	1.11
Trial 2	0.79
Trial 3	0.97
Trial 4	0.80
Trial 5	0.82

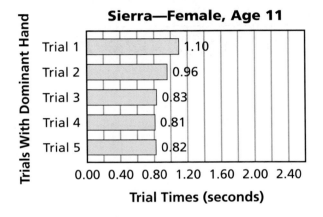

Sierra—Female, Age 11

Trials With Dominant Hand

Trial	Trial Times (seconds)
Trial 1	1.10
Trial 2	0.96
Trial 3	0.83
Trial 4	0.81
Trial 5	0.82

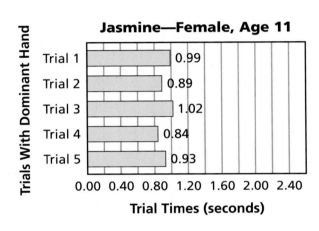

Jasmine—Female, Age 11

Trials With Dominant Hand

Trial	Trial Times (seconds)
Trial 1	0.99
Trial 2	0.89
Trial 3	1.02
Trial 4	0.84
Trial 5	0.93

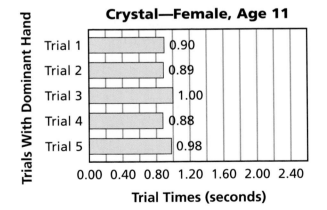

Crystal—Female, Age 11

Trials With Dominant Hand

Trial	Trial Times (seconds)
Trial 1	0.90
Trial 2	0.89
Trial 3	1.00
Trial 4	0.88
Trial 5	0.98

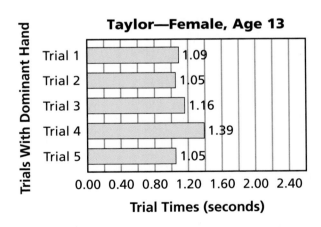

Taylor—Female, Age 13

Trials With Dominant Hand

Trial	Trial Times (seconds)
Trial 1	1.09
Trial 2	1.05
Trial 3	1.16
Trial 4	1.39
Trial 5	1.05

Reaction Time Cards

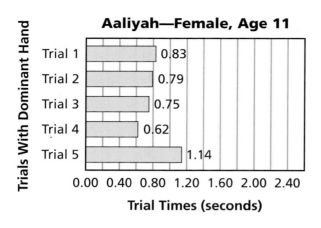

Aaliyah—Female, Age 11

Trials With Dominant Hand

Trial	Time
Trial 1	0.83
Trial 2	0.79
Trial 3	0.75
Trial 4	0.62
Trial 5	1.14

Trial Times (seconds)

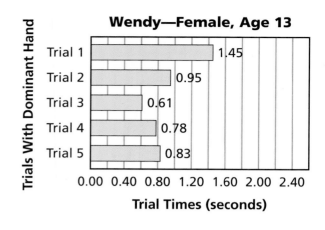

Wendy—Female, Age 13

Trials With Dominant Hand

Trial	Time
Trial 1	1.45
Trial 2	0.95
Trial 3	0.61
Trial 4	0.78
Trial 5	0.83

Trial Times (seconds)

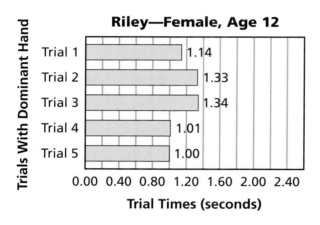

Riley—Female, Age 12

Trials With Dominant Hand

Trial	Time
Trial 1	1.14
Trial 2	1.33
Trial 3	1.34
Trial 4	1.01
Trial 5	1.00

Trial Times (seconds)

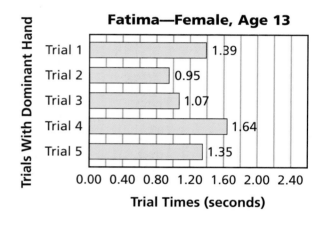

Fatima—Female, Age 13

Trials With Dominant Hand

Trial	Time
Trial 1	1.39
Trial 2	0.95
Trial 3	1.07
Trial 4	1.64
Trial 5	1.35

Trial Times (seconds)

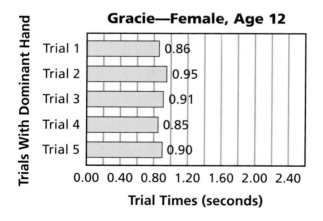

Gracie—Female, Age 12

Trials With Dominant Hand

Trial	Time
Trial 1	0.86
Trial 2	0.95
Trial 3	0.91
Trial 4	0.85
Trial 5	0.90

Trial Times (seconds)

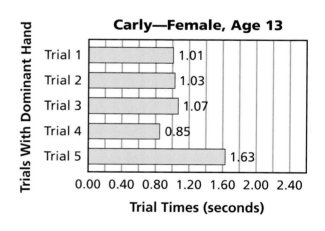

Carly—Female, Age 13

Trials With Dominant Hand

Trial	Time
Trial 1	1.01
Trial 2	1.03
Trial 3	1.07
Trial 4	0.85
Trial 5	1.63

Trial Times (seconds)

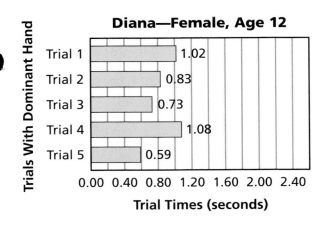

Diana—Female, Age 12

Trials With Dominant Hand / Trial Times (seconds)

- Trial 1: 1.02
- Trial 2: 0.83
- Trial 3: 0.73
- Trial 4: 1.08
- Trial 5: 0.59

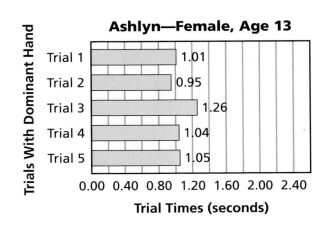

Ashlyn—Female, Age 13

Trials With Dominant Hand / Trial Times (seconds)

- Trial 1: 1.01
- Trial 2: 0.95
- Trial 3: 1.26
- Trial 4: 1.04
- Trial 5: 1.05

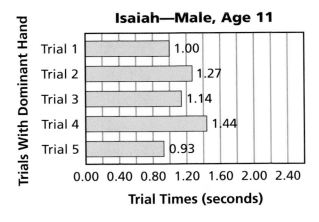

Isaiah—Male, Age 11

Trials With Dominant Hand / Trial Times (seconds)

- Trial 1: 1.00
- Trial 2: 1.27
- Trial 3: 1.14
- Trial 4: 1.44
- Trial 5: 0.93

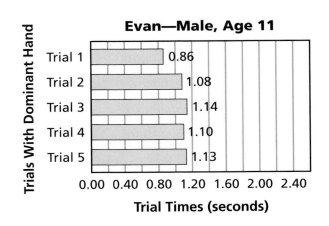

Evan—Male, Age 11

Trials With Dominant Hand / Trial Times (seconds)

- Trial 1: 0.86
- Trial 2: 1.08
- Trial 3: 1.14
- Trial 4: 1.10
- Trial 5: 1.13

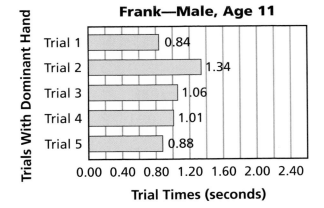

Frank—Male, Age 11

Trials With Dominant Hand / Trial Times (seconds)

- Trial 1: 0.84
- Trial 2: 1.34
- Trial 3: 1.06
- Trial 4: 1.01
- Trial 5: 0.88

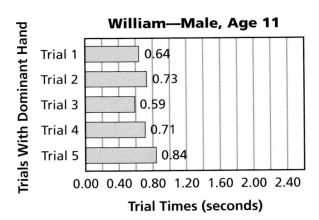

William—Male, Age 11

Trials With Dominant Hand / Trial Times (seconds)

- Trial 1: 0.64
- Trial 2: 0.73
- Trial 3: 0.59
- Trial 4: 0.71
- Trial 5: 0.84

Reaction Time Cards

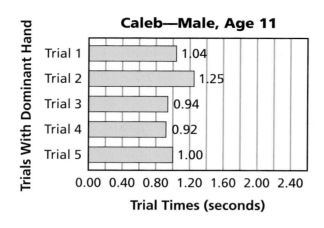

Caleb—Male, Age 11

Trials With Dominant Hand / Trial Times (seconds)

Trial 1: 1.04
Trial 2: 1.25
Trial 3: 0.94
Trial 4: 0.92
Trial 5: 1.00

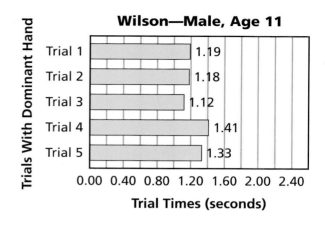

Wilson—Male, Age 11

Trials With Dominant Hand / Trial Times (seconds)

Trial 1: 1.19
Trial 2: 1.18
Trial 3: 1.12
Trial 4: 1.41
Trial 5: 1.33

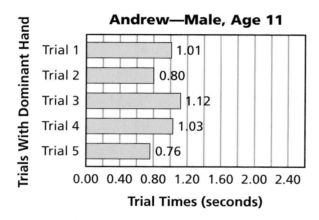

Andrew—Male, Age 11

Trials With Dominant Hand / Trial Times (seconds)

Trial 1: 1.01
Trial 2: 0.80
Trial 3: 1.12
Trial 4: 1.03
Trial 5: 0.76

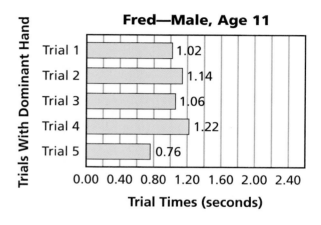

Fred—Male, Age 11

Trials With Dominant Hand / Trial Times (seconds)

Trial 1: 1.02
Trial 2: 1.14
Trial 3: 1.06
Trial 4: 1.22
Trial 5: 0.76

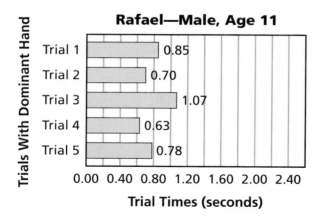

Rafael—Male, Age 11

Trials With Dominant Hand / Trial Times (seconds)

Trial 1: 0.85
Trial 2: 0.70
Trial 3: 1.07
Trial 4: 0.63
Trial 5: 0.78

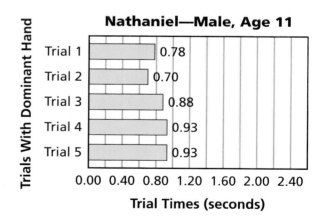

Nathaniel—Male, Age 11

Trials With Dominant Hand / Trial Times (seconds)

Trial 1: 0.78
Trial 2: 0.70
Trial 3: 0.88
Trial 4: 0.93
Trial 5: 0.93

Michael—Male, Age 11

Trials With Dominant Hand

Trial 1	0.73
Trial 2	0.73
Trial 3	0.96
Trial 4	0.80
Trial 5	1.22

Trial Times (seconds)

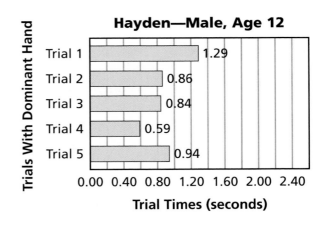

Hayden—Male, Age 12

Trials With Dominant Hand

Trial 1	1.29
Trial 2	0.86
Trial 3	0.84
Trial 4	0.59
Trial 5	0.94

Trial Times (seconds)

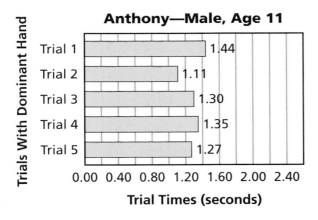

Anthony—Male, Age 11

Trials With Dominant Hand

Trial 1	1.44
Trial 2	1.11
Trial 3	1.30
Trial 4	1.35
Trial 5	1.27

Trial Times (seconds)

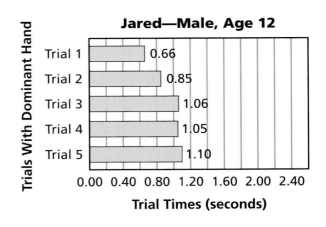

Jared—Male, Age 12

Trials With Dominant Hand

Trial 1	0.66
Trial 2	0.85
Trial 3	1.06
Trial 4	1.05
Trial 5	1.10

Trial Times (seconds)

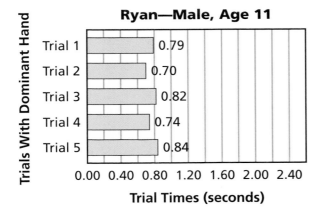

Ryan—Male, Age 11

Trials With Dominant Hand

Trial 1	0.79
Trial 2	0.70
Trial 3	0.82
Trial 4	0.74
Trial 5	0.84

Trial Times (seconds)

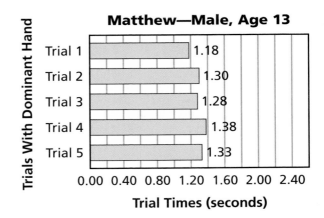

Matthew—Male, Age 13

Trials With Dominant Hand

Trial 1	1.18
Trial 2	1.30
Trial 3	1.28
Trial 4	1.38
Trial 5	1.33

Trial Times (seconds)

Reaction Time Cards

Jeremy—Male, Age 12

Trials With Dominant Hand

Trial 1: 0.85
Trial 2: 0.85
Trial 3: 1.10
Trial 4: 0.67
Trial 5: 0.61

Trial Times (seconds)

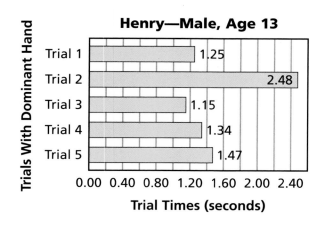

Henry—Male, Age 13

Trials With Dominant Hand

Trial 1: 1.25
Trial 2: 2.48
Trial 3: 1.15
Trial 4: 1.34
Trial 5: 1.47

Trial Times (seconds)

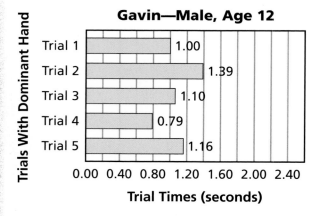

Gavin—Male, Age 12

Trials With Dominant Hand

Trial 1: 1.00
Trial 2: 1.39
Trial 3: 1.10
Trial 4: 0.79
Trial 5: 1.16

Trial Times (seconds)

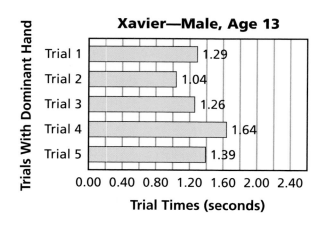

Xavier—Male, Age 13

Trials With Dominant Hand

Trial 1: 1.29
Trial 2: 1.04
Trial 3: 1.26
Trial 4: 1.64
Trial 5: 1.39

Trial Times (seconds)

Index

Algebra
  axis, 73
  coordinate graph, 52, 53
  equation, 84
  formula, 52, 53
  graph, 13, 14, 16, 22, 24, 35–38,
    40, 41, 45, 52, 58, 63, 67-69,
    71, 73, 83, 86, 88
  line, 26, 52, 53, 84
  ratio, 55, 56, 73, 80
  variable, 87
  variability, 4, 5, 13, 15, 23, 27, 28,
    30, 31, 50, 56, 57, 62, 70, 83, 86

Attribute, 89, 93

Average, *see* **Mean**

Bar graph, *see* **Value bar graph**

Case cards, *see* **Reaction time
  cards**

Categorical data, 6–8, 17, 27, 40,
    60, 70, 89
  definition, 89
  variability in, 6–8

Central angle, 67

Checking answers, 41

Circle graph, 51, 67, 72, 80
  making, 51

Circumference, 13

Cluster, *see* **Data cluster**

Collecting data, 5–6, 12–13, 75
  measurement errors and, 4,
    13–15
  measuring head sizes, 12–13

Comparing distribution, 55–85, 86
  ACE, 62–72, 78–84

Concrete model, *see* **Model**

Coordinate graph, 52–53, 86–87
  fitting a line to a, 52–53
  making, 52–53, 86

Counts, 7, 27, 76, 86, 89

Data
  categorical, 6–8, 17, 27, 40, 60,
    70, 89
  cluster, 4, 5, 12, 15, 17, 20, 25, 28,
    37–40, 48, 54, 61

  numerical, 8–13, 17, 27, 37, 40,
    54, 60, 70, 91
  outliers, 12, 15, 17, 25, 28, 70, 90,
    92

Data cluster, 4, 5, 12, 15, 28, 37–40,
    54, 61
  ACE, 17, 20, 25, 48

Distribution, 4–88, 89
  ACE, 16–26, 44–53, 62–72,
    78–84
  comparing, 55–85, 86
  definition, 89
  of equal numbers of data
    values, 55–73, 85, 88
  repeated values and, 36–40
  shape of, 4, 40–43, 49, 54, 58, 66,
    83, 88
  of unequal numbers of data
    values, 74–85, 88

Equation, writing, 53, 84

Formula, 52, 53

Frequency, 6

Fulcrum, 32, 37

Glossary, 89–94

Graph
  circle, 51, 67, 72, 80
  coordinate, 52–53, 86–87
  definition, 89
  ordered value bar, 14–15, 92
  value bar, 7–11, 13–16, 18–20,
    22, 27, 30, 36–38, 48, 50,
    56–62, 66–69, 71, 73, 75, 78,
    83, 86, 88, 89, 92–101

Interpreting data
  circle graph, 51, 67, 72, 80
  coordinate graph, 52–53, 86–87
  line plot, 14–15, 17, 20, 23, 24,
    33–35, 38–41, 44–47, 50,
    63–67, 69, 71, 73, 77, 79, 83,
    90
  picture, 29, 52, 81
  scatter plot, 26, 84, 89, 93
  stem–and–leaf plot, 21–23
  table, 7–8, 10–11, 13, 15–16, 18,
    20, 23–24, 27, 31, 33, 44–45,
    50, 53, 56–57, 65, 75–77, 78,
    80, 82–83, 87

  value bar graph, 7–11, 13–16,
    18–20, 22, 27, 30, 36–38, 48,
    50, 56–62, 66–69, 71, 73, 75,
    78, 83, 86, 88, 89, 92–101

Investigation
  Comparing Distributions:
    Equal Numbers of Data
    Values, 55–73
  Comparing Distributions:
    Unequal Numbers of Data
    Values, 74–85
  Making Sense of Measures of
    Center, 28–54
  Making Sense of Variability,
    5–27

Justify answer, 5, 8, 12–13, 15,
    30–31, 35, 37–39, 41, 43, 54,
    59–61, 73, 76–77, 85–88
  ACE, 16–17, 19–20, 23, 25–26,
    44–47, 49–53, 62–66, 69,
    79–83

Justify method, 27, 34, 38–39, 54,
    58–59, 85, 88
  ACE, 17, 20, 51, 72

Line, 26, 52, 53, 84

Line plot, 14–15, 33–35, 38–41,
    73, 77, 90
  ACE, 17, 20, 23, 24, 44–47, 50,
    63–67, 69, 71, 79, 83
  making, 12, 15, 20, 23, 33–34,
    44, 46–47, 50, 69

**Looking Back and Looking
  Ahead: Unit Review,** 86–88

Manipulatives
  fulcrum simulation, 32–33

Mathematical Highlights, 4

Mathematical Reflections, 27,
    54, 73, 85

Mean, 4, 28–35, 37, 39–43, 54,
    58–59, 61, 77, 85, 88, 90
  ACE, 44–51, 62, 64, 66–67,
    69, 81, 83
  as the average, 29, 51, 90
  as a balance point, 32–35, 54,
    85, 90
  as an equal share, 29–31, 54, 85,
    90

compared to median, 45, 49, 54, 58, 69
definition, 29, 90
shape of the distribution and, 4, 40–43, 49, 54, 58, 66, 83, 88

Measures, 90

Measures of center, 28–54, 57, 86, 89–90
ACE, 44–53
definition, 28
mean, 4, 28–35, 37, 39–43, 54, 58–59, 61, 77, 85, 88, 90
median, 4, 28, 37–38, 40–43, 54, 59, 61, 77, 85, 88, 91
mode, 28, 36, 38–40, 54, 91

Median, 4, 28, 37–38, 40–43, 54, 59, 61, 77, 85, 88, 91
ACE, 23, 45–47, 49–50, 62, 64, 66–67, 69, 71, 81, 83
compared to mean, 45, 49, 54, 58, 69
definition, 37, 91
shape of the distribution and, 4, 40–43, 49, 54, 58, 66, 83, 88

Mode, 28, 36, 38–40, 54, 91
ACE, 23, 48–49, 66
definition, 36, 91

Model
circle graph, 72, 80
coordinate graph, 87
line plot, 14, 17, 20, 23, 33–35, 38–41, 45–47, 63–67, 71, 79, 83, 90
picture, 29, 52, 81
scatter plot, 26, 84, 93
stem-and-leaf plot, 21–22
value bar graph, 7, 9–11, 13–14, 18–19, 22, 30, 36–38, 48, 56–58, 62, 66–68, 71, 92, 94, 95–101

Notebook, 27, 54, 73, 85

Numerical data, 8–13, 17, 27, 37, 40, 54, 60, 70, 91
definition, 91
variability in, 8–13

Ordered value bar graph (*see also* **Value bar graph),** 14–15, 92

Outliers, 12, 15, 17, 25, 28, 70, 90, 92
definition, 28, 92

Pattern, looking for, 8, 11, 16, 22, 27, 69–70

Pictorial model, *see* **Model**

Picture, 29, 52, 81

Problem-solving strategies
checking answers, 41
collecting data, 5–6, 12–13, 75
looking for a pattern, 8, 11, 16, 22, 27, 69–70
making a circle graph, 51
making a coordinate graph, 52–53, 86
making a line plot, 12, 15, 20, 23, 33–34, 44, 46–47, 50, 69
making a scatter plot, 26, 84
making a stem-and-leaf plot, 23
making a table, 75
making a value bar graph, 8, 11, 15–16, 18–20, 50, 59, 75, 78, 83, 86
writing an equation, 53, 84
writing a statement, 8, 11, 13, 15, 16, 19, 22–23, 26, 30–31, 38–39, 44, 56, 61–64, 71–72, 75–76, 78–80, 83

Range, 12, 15, 27, 30–31, 34, 37, 59, 61, 77, 85, 92, 94
ACE, 17, 20, 25, 49, 62, 64
definition, 28, 92

Ratio, 55, 56, 73, 80

Reaction time cards, 60, 95–99

Repeated values, 36–40

Scatter plot, 26, 84, 89, 93
fitting a line to, 26, 84
making, 26, 84

Shape of the distribution, 4, 54, 58, 88
ACE, 40–43, 49, 66, 83
estimating and, 4, 83
mean and, 4, 40–43, 49, 54, 58, 66, 83, 88
median and, 4, 40–43, 49, 54, 58, 66, 83, 88

Stem-and-leaf plot, 21–23
making, 23

Table, 7–8, 10–11, 13, 15, 27, 31, 33, 56–57, 75–77, 87
ACE, 16, 18, 20, 23–24, 44–45, 50, 53, 65, 78, 80, 82–83
making, 75

Value bar graph, 7–11, 13–15, 27, 30, 36–38, 56–61, 73, 75, 86, 88, 89, 92–101
ACE, 16, 18–20, 22, 48, 50, 62, 66–69, 71, 78, 83
making, 8, 11, 15–16, 18–20, 50, 59, 75, 78, 83, 86
ordered, 14–15, 92

Value of an attribute, 93

Variable, 87

Variability, 4–88, 94
ACE, 16–26, 44–53, 62–72, 78–84
definition, 5, 94
measurement errors and, 4, 13–15

Writing a statement, 8, 11, 13, 15, 30–31, 38–39, 56, 61, 75–76
ACE, 16, 19, 22–23, 26, 44, 62–64, 71–72, 78–80, 83

Acknowledgments

Team Credits

The people who made up the **Connected Mathematics 2** team—representing editorial, editorial services, design services, and production services—are listed below. Bold type denotes core team members.

Leora Adler, Judith Buice, Kerry Cashman, Patrick Culleton, Sheila DeFazio, Richard Heater, **Barbara Hollingdale, Jayne Holman,** Karen Holtzman, **Etta Jacobs,** Christine Lee, Carolyn Lock, Catherine Maglio, **Dotti Marshall,** Rich McMahon, Eve Melnechuk, Kristin Mingrone, Terri Mitchell, **Marsha Novak,** Irene Rubin, Donna Russo, Robin Samper, Siri Schwartzman, **Nancy Smith,** Emily Soltanoff, **Mark Tricca,** Paula Vergith, Roberta Warshaw, Helen Young

Additional Credits

Diana Bonfilio, Mairead Reddin, Michael Torocsik, nSight, Inc.

Technical Illustration

WestWords, Inc.

Cover Design

tom white.images

Photographs

Every effort has been made to secure permission and provide appropriate credit for photographic material. The publisher deeply regrets any omission and pledges to correct errors called to its attention in subsequent editions.

Unless otherwise acknowledged, all photographs are the property of Pearson Education, Inc.

Photo locators denoted as follows: Top (T), Center (C), Bottom (B), Left (L), Right (R), Background (Bkgd)

2 (T) picturesbyrob/Alamy, (C) Gail Mooney/Masterfile Corporation, (B) Cheryl Hatch/©Associated Press; **3** RNT Productions/Corbis; **5** Chad Slattery/Getty Images; **6** Exactostock/SuperStock; **11** (B) Jonathan Nourok/PhotoEdit, Inc.; **19** (B) Bob Daemmrich/The Image Works, Inc.; **21** (B) Ryan McVay/Photodisc/Getty Images; **23** (B) David Young-Wolff/PhotoEdit, Inc.; **25** Denis Kuvaev/Shutterstock; **28** Matthew Stockman/ Getty Images; **36** Chris Collins/Corbis; **37** Gail Mooney/Masterfile Corporation; **49** Dylan Martinez/Corbis; **52** (T) M.T. Frazier/Photo Researchers, Inc.; **55** Spencer Grant/PhotoEdit, Inc.; **58** MedioImages/Digital Vision/Getty Images; **61** Cheryl Hatch/©Associated Press; **63** Richard Hutchings/PhotoEdit, Inc.; **69** image100/Getty Images; **74** Jeff Greenberg/ PhotoEdit, Inc.; **78** Gail Mooney/Masterfile Corporation; **84** Lester Lefkowitz/Getty Images

Data Sources

Grateful acknowledgement is made to the following for copyrighted material:

President's Council on Physical Fitness and Sports
"Qualifying Standards for the Presidential and National Physical Fitness Award" from WWW.FITNESS.GOV (p. 24)

Acknowledgments

Data Sources (continued)

Lippincott Williams & Wilkins

"Nutritional Content of Ready to Eat Cereals" by Jean A. T. Pennington from BOWES AND CHURCH'S FOOD VALUES OF PORTIONS COMMONLY USED 17TH EDITION (pp 33, 38–43)

North Carolina Cooperative Extension

"Eastern Garter Snakes in North America" from WWW.CES.NESU.EDU (p 70)

MarketResearch.com

"Pizza Industry Facts" from PACKAGED FACTS. Used by permission. (p 70)

Duane Marden

"Roller Coaster Census Report" by Duane Marden from WW.RCDB.COM/CENSUS.HTM (pp 76, 80)

National Geographic Stock

"Survey 2000: Census Information" from WWW.NATIONALGEOGRAPHIC.COM. Used by permission of NGS/National Geographic Stock (p 82)